*The House*

*Where the Hardest*

*Things Happened*

# The House Where the Hardest Things Happened

A MEMOIR
ABOUT BELONGING

*Kate Young Caley*

DOUBLEDAY

NEW YORK  LONDON  TORONTO  SYDNEY  AUCKLAND

PUBLISHED BY DOUBLEDAY
a division of Random House, Inc.
1540 Broadway, New York, New York 10036

DOUBLEDAY and the portrayal of an anchor with a dolphin are
trademarks of Doubleday, a division of Random House, Inc.

*Book design by Pei Loi Koay*
Cataloging-in-Publication Data is on file with the Library of Congress

ISBN 0-385-50298-2

PRINTED IN THE UNITED STATES OF AMERICA

July 2002
First Edition

1  2  3  4  5  6  7  8  9  10

*For my mother,*

*June MacDonald Young,*

*who bravely told her stories*

*so I could tell mine*

# Contents

# Foreword

BY PHYLLIS TICKLE

Kate Caley and I share a number of things. There are friends we hold in common; there is our love of words and of fashioning them into things other than themselves; there is in both of us the sense of an all-informing gratitude that such a thing as the Episcopal Church exists and that, existing, it has accepted us into its ample and liturgy-drenched embrace. Beyond all these things, we share a literary agent, Joseph Durepos.

I was talking to Joe not long ago about my deep pleasure in the manuscript of *The House Where the Hardest Things Happened.* "Yes," he said in response to my rather general comments, "but mainly, I think, it's a book about saying good-bye to things bitter and sweet, and about finding one's way back home."

Joe's words have stayed with me since that afternoon, because in them, as is the way of a good agent, he has caught in one perfect, still frame of a sentence, the elusive and redeeming poignancy that dances through these pages . . . and this is a redemptive book. Let there be no mistake about that.

This is the story of a child's love that was violated by both a congregation and a township; just as it is the story as well of how those wounds were soothed by another congregation and another place. Important as both these things are, however, above them and binding them is another story, the story of one woman's progress toward that maturity of soul which accepts and forgives and then, in doing so, finds itself on its way back home at last.

*I was glad when they*

*said unto me,*

*"Let us go into the*

*house of the Lord!"*

PSALM 122:1

# Introduction

ONE NIGHT AS I WAS FALLING ASLEEP, I was thinking about who gets to belong and who doesn't. I was thinking about my Dad. Though he has been dead for ten years, he is so much a part of me I sometimes forget he is gone. I was thinking about all the crazy things he did in his life. I thought, "I wonder what he was looking for?" Perhaps, it was God.

And me, the daughter of this searching man—what have I been looking for? Is it the grace of belonging I still seek? How I have always yearned for that.

There are ways that my need to belong has been deeply satisfied over the years. I have been married for twenty years. The lastingness of me and Roy Caley is a central place in my life out of which I live and become. I am the mother of our children. I, who grew up wanting a sister, got daughters. And that keeps amazing me.

Yet there are ways that I carry a lingering, sad sense of not belonging.

Where do I come from? Who am I now? Those were my thoughts in the days leading up to the surgery.

I sat in a small and curtained cubicle, my husband holding my hand. Trying not to show his nervousness. My beloved friend, Ruthanne, was with us. If she could not go into that operating room herself (which in her tough, redheadedness I am sure she would have preferred), she could at least stand at the door outside, and implore God to pay attention.

I was cold in the thin johnny the nurse had handed me. I placed my hand on the lump I had felt growing for months. No more pretending it wasn't there. It was time to face what it meant.

An attendant rolled my stretcher into a room where it was just me and a team of people who did not know me. No husband. No friend.

Attendants strapped me down to the table at my feet and waist and chest. My hands were outstretched on either side, needled with tubes, and the lights above me were so bright I had to close my eyes.

They were all so busy, these people who did not know me. I would have liked to have a little visit first. Maybe a joke. But one of them came at me with a mask and told me to breathe in, breathe in. I didn't want to because if I did, I'd sleep—and it was while I was sleeping that it would be decided if I would get my life or not.

*I want to live. That is my prayer. To be my daughters' mother. To belong to the land of the living. That's the only thing I ask. I'll do anything. Don't take me away from them.*

And it was in that moment strapped down, not unlike Christ, that I realized there was not one single thing I could do. Around me, the busy people scurried and prepared to open me up for the answer. I breathed in and breathed out. "Abba, Father, I belong to you," I whispered. Then I went under.

When I awoke my life, thank you God, was still there. I got to go home, like well people do, and be busy, and calm, and amazed, and bored. I got to live.

But the experience changed me. I could no longer fool myself about mortality. I could not assume, any more, that there would be time for the stories I wanted to tell. I decided there were things I want to be sure my daughters knew about my life.

I want them to know where I came from. Not just the town. But all of the circumstances. It is hard for my children to comprehend that I am anything but their mother, at this current age. But I need to try to tell them who I also am. And have been.

The proof I might have used to tell them about my past is disappearing. I've no evidence of the places or the people, other than my words.

My father is gone. The farm where I grew up is gone. The fields and brooks I played in have all been developed with brand-new houses, one after the other. My girls do not know certain things that happened to their uncles (my brothers Peter and Richie) and me. Things I think they need to understand so that they will know better how to be in this life. But there is no proof of what we were. No proof of how we've struggled to find our place.

I want to save what I can and put it down on paper so they can begin to know what I have known. So they can be changed by it.

For me, it all began in the granite hills of New Hampshire, where the mountains and the people and the life can be hard. I remember it this way.

# CHAPTER ONE

# *When Everyone Loved Us*

BROTHER MUNROE IS PREACHING. I am five years old and I am sitting in my favorite place: The First Church of God in Moultonboro, New Hampshire. He is talking about how important God's Book is to him. It's important to me too. We, in the primary department, are memorizing the names of the books of the New Testament and if I recite them all, Mrs. Nichols will give me a gold necklace that has a tiny glass bulb with a mustard seed inside. That tiny seed is like the kingdom of heaven—that's what Mrs. Nichols told us—and I want the necklace so I can figure out how this could be so.

I look up from the chair where I sit and see that Brother Munroe is crying again. He cries, my mother explains, because he really believes. Then he is shouting at us, "And if you don't feel this way, then you might as well throw the whole thing out the window right now!" And as he says the words he flings his Bible out into the congregation toward the window where Althea Buckley always sits.

Maybe it is only my imagination, but the Bible seems within inches of hitting me in the face as it flies by. I wait for the smashing of glass at the window, but there is none. Brother Munroe had tied a rope around his Bible, and just as it is about to smash the windowpanes he jerks the rope and whips the Bible back to him like a cowboy in a movie.

Thirty-five years later, that sermon illustration is still working its message in me. Part of the message I keep with me is that things can happen in a church you'll never be able to forget.

Back then, the sounds of Sunday mornings were sounds that meant everything was all right. That we were all together, cleaned and dressed up. My father in his tie and jacket, handsome as a movie star. My mother, all fancy in high heels that made little holes in the dirt lot where we parked our car, with a scented cloud of Shalimar following her up the stairs. When we walked into church, everybody loved us.

Old Miss Lynch sat at the donated piano and plunked accompaniment to our love for God and each other. How could we not be moved by the towering promises of those gospel hymns? We knew every word to "There Is Power in the Blood" and "Blessed Assurance Jesus Is Mine." My parents' voices harmonized above me as I stood between them and they sang my favorite words, "My sheep know my voice . . . no danger nor harm will touch one of them, for I will be with them always." My father's voice was so deep I could feel it in my stomach and my mother's voice blended so exactly with his, you had to believe God created them only for each other.

I remember the sound of shuffling feet and scraping chairs against the cement floor as we sat down to listen to the day's sermon. Brother Henry, behind me, would pull out a butterscotch hard candy and slowly untwist the stiff cellophane. And this would remind me that I, too, was hungry and in need of diversion. I'd muffle the snap of the little metal clasp on my mother's handbag and look for my favorite—a box of pink Canada Mints. Usually, I would have to settle for a lint-covered Tums that I'd suck silently as Brother Munroe preached about redemption. I remember the sound of his fist hitting the pulpit and then the quiet, slow turn of the tissue-thin pages of his Bible that lay open in his hand, as limp as a dead hen.

As the sermon came to a close, old Miss Lynch would begin a strain of a sad song, so softly you'd barely notice at first. One or two would begin singing. A few more. Then all of us would join in on the songs that called us Home.

Every Sunday was the same. And there was such grace in sameness. But all that was before they kicked us out.

# CHAPTER TWO

# The
# Complication

MY MOTHER HAD JUST DELIVERED our baby brother, and was still bleeding the birthing blood. She seemed to cry a lot. My older brother was eight years old. I was five. And one night, my Dad did not come home.

At midnight we still hadn't heard a thing. Was he alive? Had he left us for good like the husband across the street? Did he need us and wonder why we didn't come to help? That possibility made me cry the hardest.

The next morning neighbors and friends crowded our kitchen with cups of tea and plates of sandwiches. Long distance calls were placed to Nana, my father's mother. To aunts and uncles. Another day went by. Another night. There was lots of crying and there were hushed voices and words whose meanings I did not understand, but could imagine well enough. Someone sat at the piano and played hymns. They were so achingly familiar I could hear my father's harmony in them.

I remember I sat on my parents' bed because it smelled like

them. I played with my dolls, dressing and re-dressing them; taking care of them the way I wished someone would take care of me. It was three days before we heard anything.

Amnesia. That's what the doctors called it. In February of 1965, my Dad had reported for duty to his base in Biloxi, Mississippi, certain it was 1954 and he was still in the army. They could not convince him otherwise.

"A breakdown," that's what the ladies in the kitchen whispered as they shook their heads. "It's been too much for him."

Within the last couple of years my father's younger brother had committed suicide and their father had died of a stroke. My Dad found a lump on his neck one morning while he was shaving but didn't dare to tell anyone. If you don't tell anyone about it, maybe it isn't even there.

But eventually he took himself to the doctor and when the follow-up call came, the test results were not good. The pain that had been troubling him in his throat was cancer. They told him to get his wife and come in, right away. Instead, he pawned his favorite guitar for cash, parked his truck at the bus depot, and bought a ticket to Biloxi.

Years later, my Dad told me that the strangest moment of his entire life was when the commanding officer of the base held up the front page of the daily newspaper to prove to him, after many failed attempts, the day and year it really was. My Dad said he kept looking at that date, trying to figure out how they did the joke.

He looked up at me, as I sat across from him waiting for the rest of the story. He shook his head, smiled his handsome smile, and shrugged as if he still couldn't figure it out.

When he had finally called my mother, he was sitting in the base sergeant's office. A doctor had been brought in, a couple of MPs. Someone had to come and get him, he told her. He asked if the kids were okay.

My mother asked, "You remember us, Dick?" and he said, "June, don't be ridiculous." When she got off the phone, she could not stop crying.

I realize now, how particularly young my mother was when all this happened. She was slender and small. Twenty-nine years old. She loved movie magazines and pretty bathrobes. When she vacuumed the rugs, she played her Patsy Cline record up loud and smoked a cigarette and danced the stroll as she pulled the canister across the room.

My father had talked her into eloping with him and moving from the city, where all her aunts and uncles had settled from Prince Edward Island, to a little town where she didn't know anyone. Eight years later, she was still homesick. And now he was gone.

She took weak bites of the little sandwiches the church ladies handed her, imploring her to keep up her strength for the children. My mother's mother arrived. Neighbors brought more food. We all waited together.

Uncle Frannie and Uncle George drove to Mississippi to bring my father back to us. But it didn't turn out to be so simple.

Nana, my father's mother, had made arrangements for him to be admitted to a state mental hospital near where she lived in the city. She implied the trouble was all my mother's fault. The doctor insisted my mother sign the papers to admit my father. My father cried and begged her not to do it. The doctor said there was no choice. What else could my mother do?

Could she have said, "Nana, do you know the real trouble? That he only stutters when he is with you? That he has to stop the car and *throw up* before we get to your house, Nana—your house with all that fine, family silver?"

But my mother was not that way. And now it's too late. So

many of them are gone. The doctor. Nana. My Dad. So what does it matter? Still, I ask my questions to try to understand what happened to us back then. And my mother tries to answer. We work at it. And when the words are hard to find, we wait. It's work she understands I have to do.

# CHAPTER THREE

# After The First Church of God

AFTER THE TIME HE SPENT in the psychiatric ward, my Dad was treated for his cancer at the Veteran's Administration Hospital in White River Junction, near the border between New Hampshire and Vermont. In those days, people with cancer were hospitalized for months. We drove each Sunday afternoon over the winding roads in our unreliable car that pumped exhaust into the back seat and made our stomachs and heads hurt. It was a long ride for my brothers and me, who sat, tired and cranky, cramped together.

When we finally got to him each week, my father was not the same man we knew. He was quiet. He was thin. He seemed more comfortable among pale men in faded johnnies playing sad hands of solitaire than he did with us. His neck was burned from radiation. That redness never did fade.

Ultimately, though, the cancer treatments worked and my father came back to us. He was shaky and weak, and so were we really; but when we tell the story of those years, we always end with this: He was the only man on his ward who lived.

And though he survived when the doctors said he would die—causing us to confuse him slightly, but forever, with that other immortal, invincible Father we revered—we never did get our old life back. That one I had loved, where my Dad had just become a minister of the church. Where he stood in the pulpit preaching with his deep voice. And I sat proudly in the front row.

Over the months he was away from us in the hospital, my mother had taken a job as a waitress. It was the best job she could find in our small town, serving dinner in a fancy place that catered to the tourists who owned expensive property on the nearby lakes. My mother was friendly. The tips were good. But when word spread to The First Church of God, there was trouble.

The problem was this: my mother was serving alcohol and though she didn't drink herself, that wasn't the point. When my father got out of the hospital, a meeting was called. My parents sat in their usual pew. A vote of the congregation was taken. Hands raised in vote all around them. The numbers were clear. June Young had broken the covenant. She had to leave. And my father walked out the door with her.

Because she thought it the right thing to do, my mother still dropped my older brother and me off at Sunday school each week, waiting in the car while we learned our Bible stories. She didn't want us to have to miss out on church just because she couldn't be there.

Then one morning my teacher told the class that my mother was a bad woman. She used her as an example of sin for our lesson that day. I remember asking my mother, "What does hypocrite mean?" She couldn't find a way to answer. I started to cry. She set her jaw. That was the last Sunday we went.

And so I, who loved church—who was so close to having memorized the names of all the books of the New Testament, so close to earning the mustard seed necklace and the kingdom of heaven, itself—I too was out.

Over the years I would sometimes ask my father, "So what was it, exactly, that happened?"

And my father would say, "We broke the covenant. They voted us out." And the way he said it—short answer, deep voice, heavy, certain punctuation—made it sound like that was a sufficient explanation. Covenant. Voted. Out. It was never enough for me, that answer. But I didn't know how to get any other.

I remember that covenant. It stated the rules that church members had to agree to abide by. It was written on a muslin cloth that hung behind the pulpit. There were big Roman numerals and words stenciled with heavy black paint. Certain words were done with red paint to make them stand out, but since I could not yet read, I did not know why. I only knew that there were words on that muslin cloth that made it okay to make my mother cry. And to make me cry too.

A few months after we got kicked out, I was standing in the bread aisle at Ellen's General Store. I was looking up and down the shelf for the bright colors of our favorite brand and as I turned the corner, I looked right in the face of my Sunday school teacher, Mrs. Esther Nichols. She blushed. And with a slight tremor of—what was it—embarrassment? Disgust? (Might it have been shame?) She turned and walked away.

What had just happened? I had almost said hello. Smiled. I did not yet understand that I was *not* supposed to be glad to see her. And then I was afraid that someone else might have seen her turning away from me. Might agree with it even. And soon, no one in town would speak to me. Not even the ones who thought church was a waste of time.

I wondered if Mrs. Nichols was still in the store. Had I just heard her voice at the cash register saying something to the owner? I wanted to go to my mother, but to do that meant I had to walk past Mrs. Nichols.

Alone, in the bread aisle, I waited and tried not to cry.

How could I tell my mother what had happened? I was only six years old, but I knew enough had already happened to my parents. It would be mean to add one thing more. If I didn't tell them about Mrs. Nichols, it couldn't hurt them. And I was sick of people hurting my parents.

Recently, though, I've needed to talk about it. I try to sort it out. I ask my brothers what they remember. They say, it's over, why think about it now? But I need to understand the ways I still carry those early church experiences. I need to know now.

The first time I gave a copy of the early chapters of this book to my mother, I had been visiting her for several days. I had intended to give it to her sooner in the visit so we could have a few days to talk about it. But I knew I was asking her to move beyond the two sentences, "We broke the covenant. They voted us out," to a much more complicated conversation. I was asking her to help me put aside the cursory answers we'd relied on so long.

But the reality of that conversation scared me, so I waited until the last moment, before I kissed her goodnight, thinking that since I was leaving first thing in the morning I would do this part now. Tell her I wrote something. Give it to her. We could do the rest later.

In the morning when I opened the bedroom door to the living room, I saw her curled up on the couch, staring out at Red Hill. She was drinking a cup of tea and staring up at that line of trees as if there might be answers there she could decipher.

I poured myself some coffee and went to her. "Nice morning," I said as I gave her a kiss. We were quiet. That's comfortable for us. Then she said, "So, I read your piece."

"You did?" I was surprised. Not ready. I tried quickly to remember what I had said about her. About Dad. About what it was like for a six-year-old girl who got kicked out of the church she loved.

"I never knew how hard it was for you," she began. Then, I heard her choke a huge sob, "I'm sorry . . . I broke . . . the covenant!"

I stared at her. I was incredulous as I watched my mother cry and heave that old shame. I didn't know what to say.

Trying to be funny, to shock her out of it, to do *something* to change this scary moment, I said, "Oh, screw the covenant!"

"Kate!" She scolded me like a child. "Don't talk like that."

I checked myself. This was fragile and rare and important. I mustn't leave what she was saying, but stay with her. *Don't dig a hole, shove her in, and then joke about it. No, I must be with this woman.*

"Mom," I said and reached toward my crying, crying mother. "Mom," I took a breath. "It was a really bad covenant."

She looked up at me, snuffled, and wiped her wet face with the back of her hand. "It was," she said. "And none of them helped me find another way. Not one of them said, 'I'll pay those bills, you don't have to work there.' "

"Oh, Mom," I said and I could see what my need for answers had cost her and would cost us both.

So now we talk. Now that I dare to ask about it, I can't seem to stop.

"Okay, you mean Doris Brown voted you out?" I asked recently. My mother nodded. "But did she still speak to you? I mean, did she vote you out and then stop by for a cup of tea?" My mother seemed confused. I moved on. "Ginny Muzzy? On her third husband? Did she vote you out?"

"Yes!" my mother said and I saw I'd awakened something in her. "And every husband with a girlfriend on the side, and every person who really did drink—but the church didn't know," she added vehemently.

Watching her hands tremble, I felt in that moment like her bodyguard. I am several inches taller than my mother, and stronger by far. I can lift my mother and sometimes, when I hug her, I feel I might squash her with my largeness. But now I feel my strong self running interference on this big, complicated field, opening a path for her to find her way across, and I will go with her.

"Mom," I said calling her back from her thoughts to me. "Your husband was just diagnosed with cancer. They told you he wouldn't live. You had three little kids. You were hemorrhaging. No money. Twenty-nine years old, Mom—that's a *girl*." I shuddered and heard myself pleading. "Did nobody see how wrong it was?"

I found myself losing my breath. It was not like I was sitting beside my mother in the house where she lives alone, years after my father died. It was as if it was thirty-five years ago and I was in the newly finished sanctuary of The First Church of God in Moultonboro, New Hampshire. And I am there, as the woman I am now. I am my mother's only protector. And I am not going to stand for any of this.

"God," I call out. "Mrs. Nichols, Ginny Muzzy, somebody—please, listen to me." I am crying. "Don't kick my mother out. Please. There are some things we are *never* going to find again."

# CHAPTER FOUR

# Saving What We Could

IT WAS AROUND THIS TIME we moved to the place that would become the landscape I would rely on all my life. I read somewhere recently that for each person there is an event in childhood that forever marks the life. For me, it was moving to my father's farm.

I call it my father's farm because it was his dream, not my mother's. He had left the church he loved when they kicked out his wife, and had been told by the doctors at the big hospital across the state line that the cancer in his body was terminal.

But then he survived. Three years later, they declared him, miraculously, cancer-free. And so we moved to my father's particular version of Eden.

It had been Martha and Peter Larson's farm, where they raised their chickens and tended neatly planned apple orchards. My Dad wasn't much of a farmer, my mother even less so, but we moved there anyway.

I still don't know how they managed to scrape together the

down payment, but when my father set his mind to it, he could make things happen. He had decided that brooks and ponds and fields and coops and sheds and an enormous main barn were just what we all needed to get our lives back. In many ways, he was right.

What I remember about that house where I grew up is a huge hunk of granite that served as a front step and the squeaking rub of the oak door against the threshold. I remember the living room woodstove, so hot when it was really stoked, you couldn't sit in the same room.

But I have forgotten things too.

I forget the words to the songs my father sang, over and over, with his country and western band, The Woodsville Ramblers, as my brothers and I tried to fall asleep at night.

I forget what year it was when my father came home with a Mexican burro that someone was giving away on his favorite radio show, "Swap-Shop." I forget the year, but I remember my mother's reaction when she saw the burro. How she did not even look up from her cigarette and cup of tea, but just stared out the window. And the way her hand shook.

I forget the taste of the rhubarb that grew in our back yard. But I recall the gigantic leaves and stalks, two and a half feet long, and how I once lay under them just to see what the sun looked like shining through those leaves.

And I remember, clearly, the feel of my hand in my father's as we walked past that rhubarb, down to the pond, my Dad and me, with a fistful of cracked corn for the mallards that were his favorite. And I remember thinking that my father was going to make everything come out okay even if people wouldn't speak to us.

It was just us. Mom. Dad. My brothers and me. And the farm. For a long while, it was enough.

. . .

My Dad embraced the farm the way he embraced everything in life—fully. He never seemed to be able to do something part way. And it made you love him if you were his kid. It made you crazy if you were his wife.

He bought a couple of Herefords, we named Millie and Martha for the two sisters buried in the little family cemetery at the edge of the orchard. These cows were intended to fill our freezer with fresh meat, but we became so attached to them they lived with us for many years as a lazy, calming presence.

He bought an old bay mare for us kids to ride through the orchards, and a pregnant sheep, just so we could watch it give birth. Moose Evans gave him ninety-nine chickens for free. Thinking that an egg business was a good way for kids to learn about money, my father excitedly brought them home.

It would have been a great idea if we had any serious layers in the group of hens. Most days, we were lucky to get two or three eggs.

My Dad sent away to a catalogue company all the way in California (that magical state where things happened faster than they did here) for fertilized quail eggs. We helped him build the incubators that filled one end of our large farm kitchen. We rigged brooders with light bulbs, wrapped in grid wire, to keep the chicks warm. We sent away to another catalogue for metal food dishes with small holes for their tiny beaks, and waterers that burbled.

My Dad got up those nights to turn the warming eggs. We waited. On our first attempt, out of two dozen eggs, we got one quail. Oh, but what a quail! We watched for hours as he pecked his way around and out of his tiny shell. We wanted so much to help him, to break it open. It would have been so easy. We begged my father to let us reach into the warm compartment and speed things up. "You'll ruin the bird if you do," he warned. A bird had to do it itself, or it wouldn't know how to survive.

I stood as an omnipotent god, watching, able to help, but not doing a thing. I was wary of such influential power but trusted my father. We waited some more.

Hours later, exhausted and wet, our one lone quail shook off his egg and peered out at us. My father reached his huge hand in to lift the bird, not much bigger than an acorn, into the brooder for its first sip of water. "Hello, Lonesome," my Dad said, smiling, and held the little creature right up to his face. "You done good."

Lonesome lived a good long quail life. We kept him in our kitchen that first spring (pecking at our cereal bowls as we ate breakfast each morning) and later, when our experiments with eggs and incubators proved more successful, with a covey of various quail, grouse, and doves in a big barn room. We rigged the pen with apple branches and pine boughs for the birds to hide in, and fly from floor to limb.

Though we would come to have hundreds of birds, a few cows, pigs, and a goat and horse here and there, Lonesome was always my Dad's favorite. I think he loved him because Lonesome, like my Dad, survived.

Or maybe I am placing my meaning on things he never really thought through. What I know is this: when we stood around the brooder that night watching that bird get itself hatched, my father was teaching us something important about how you start a new life. You do it slowly, and bit by bit, and you just have to wait it through while it happens. He knew it, and we were learning it, and the fact that none of us said anything didn't take away from the lesson. Not even a little.

.  .  .

My father read that our part of the state used to be full of wild turkeys. He sent away for some eggs, dozens and dozens of them, and once they arrived he set about the tedious incubator schedule of turning and adjusting, turning and adjusting. Twenty-eight days later, we had turkeys. Nearly a hundred. My mother protested that her kitchen smelled like the barn and so we built yet another pen, outside.

The young turkeys grew quickly. We weren't allowed to go see them much, though, because my father was trying to keep them wild. He and his best friend, Ding Martin, were determined to repopulate our state with its native bird.

The morning we let them go had long been planned and anticipated. We got up early and went out to the barn. My Dad lifted the wooden door, and he and Ding moved through the pen with brooms shooing the turkeys out.

A turkey is not a smart bird. Or maybe they were smarter than we were. They knew where to get their two meals a day. Maybe they weren't ready for the beautiful New Hampshire woods that my Dad and Ding offered.

Our job was to run them off our land into the woods across the road. My brothers and I ran all morning, chasing birds, laughing, yelling, and trying like crazy to get them to go, while Ding and my Dad stood smoking near the stonewall, laughing at us all.

A couple of weeks later, Sam Perkins, the fish and game warden, pulled into our driveway in his dark green Fish and Game truck. "Good morning, Dick," he said stepping out. "I wonder if you know anything about these turkey sightings we've been hearing about?"

"Turkeys? No kidding? Isn't that something," my Dad said. He stood there looking concerned and serious, right into the eyes of that Fish and Game guy, as the turkeys that just wouldn't leave us sat on the branches of our apple trees.

"You know what we're talking about would be illegal, right?" Mr. Perkins asked.

"Yes, I can see that it would," my father replied.

"Well, I guess that's it then," Mr. Perkins said, and climbed back into his truck and drove away. My father watched the truck pull out of the yard, and looked at the turkeys and then at us kids. He smiled. We were starting to see that with truth there was not just one way. And we were also beginning to see that starting anew, when you weren't so sure you could, was one way we might all survive.

# CHAPTER FIVE

# At the Edge of a Brook, At the Door of a Barn

HALFWAY BROOK WRAPPED AROUND our farmland, clear and cold, even in the middle of August when my brothers and I would wade through the meadow of goldenrod, black-eyed Susans, and Queen Anne's lace to the brook's sudden edge.

Our brook flowed all the way from some mountain, my father said, from so far up, from so tiny a source, we probably couldn't find it. And it ran from that place (somewhere near the stars I imagined) connecting our land to our neighbor's down the road, across wide fields, and out to Lake Winnipesaukee, and maybe even to the ocean.

Meandering shallow, over silk bottom sand, shiny with mica, the brook would suddenly pick up power—for no good reason you could see—and crash into a jumble of rocks and foam. Then it quieted again at a curve of birch, the roots curled around the water's edge in a gentle arc of wood and stones gripped with moss. I spent many hours by that brook.

Across the road from our land, on the Roths' property, was

a clearing in the woods with an abandoned sap house. I tried to find a way into it—always looking for a place to call my own—but there was no way without breaking a window. I was afraid to do that. I wasn't sure about the rules.

Near the edge of the brook I made a fort between two golden birches. I had never seen golden birch, only the white ones, common in our town. These seemed so special to me that I wondered if I was the only one who could see them. The ground was cushioned with pine needles and moss. It was my very own place. Sometimes the sun was so bright on my face, and so warm—even in November—I wondered if the bright warmth was God speaking to me.

I was wondering about where to find God in those years. Certainly it was God I sensed in the quiet by the pond where the frogs floated in the mucky water and occasionally called out their love for the summer day. But I missed church. The love I developed for the woods and the farm wasn't enough for me.

As much as I needed those places, it was so hard to get used to the long, empty hours of Sunday mornings with no more church: no Sunday school teachers who loved me, no felt-board Bible stories, no take-home craft, and no sweaty coins gathered in my palm awaiting their clunk into the offering plate. Without our church service there was silence where my father and mother's voices had once melted together in victorious song above me.

My Sunday mornings were quiet now. Empty. I was ten years old and longing for a way to find my way back to God. The church took away my right to attend. But they didn't take away my need to worship. And they couldn't take away God.

The rest of my family seemed to let go. Why couldn't I? Couldn't I have taken up Sunday morning baseball like Richie, or loved to sleep in like my tired mother? Or started to really believe in the importance of the crossword puzzle, like my father and Peter?

Why did I sit on the floor of the barn, longing for someone to harmonize with me on a hymn? Why did I think about what good Sunday school classrooms the three horse stalls would make? I could put the primaries in where we kept the pig; and divide the juniors, the big kids, into each of the stalls where our two cows and one horse stood nuzzling their feed buckets hoping for an overlooked morsel of sticky molasses feed.

Why did I make up little Jesus worksheets with fill-in-the-blanks when I had no one to give them to? And sing the Books-of-the-Bible song for fear I would forget both the tune and the content? Was I the only one who needed it all back?

Once, when he was three or four, Richie dressed up like a preacher and made us all play church. We brought chairs in from the kitchen and lined then up in the living room like pews. My grandmother and the aunts and all of us had to sit down while he preached. Then he passed a dinner plate for the collection and everyone laughed and laughed at how funny and cute he was. But was he actually missing our church? Was he sad, too?

I might ask him now, but he'd say, "Gee, why don't you let all that go?"

How do I explain I can't?

If I could figure out why those particular months of my life still feel so much like they just happened, I could understand many other things too.

# CHAPTER SIX

# Burning Back
# the Fields

HE WAS VIBRANT OR HE was ill. That's how it was with my Dad. I was a child with a sick father. And that has made it hard for me to relax. To trust.

That's one of the ways I think about my life when I am trying to figure out why I hold on so tightly.

My Dad was frequently ill. It was not just his nervous breakdown and the way that took him from our lives. It was also months of painful cancer treatments, followed by the fear associated with each checkup every eight weeks to be sure the surgeons had really gotten it all.

So much of my life was spent trying to decode, through a child's disjointed perceptions, what illness was going to mean for us. Trying to comprehend what words my father might say to my mother, quietly in another room—words we young children weren't supposed to hear—and figuring out how those words might change our lives all over again.

When I consider his many illnesses, they seem similar to our work of trying to keep brush and scrub and bull pines from overgrowing our farm. It happened so quickly, the way our land was overtaken by the insistence of surrounding woods. And it was our job to keep that threat from choking us out.

I think of the fires we burned across the fields to keep back all that insidious growth.

Burning day took place when there was no wind at all, not even the slightest bit. My father taught us to watch carefully. A fire can turn on you when you aren't looking. Never let your eyes wander.

My Dad and our friend, Bill, ready with long rakes and heavy boots, would pour a small circle of gasoline on the ground and put a match to it. Then they would work the fire inward from that little ring. Section by section they burned away the spring's new growth of brush.

My older brother and I were allowed to help with the dangerous job of stomping on fires that tried to spread. We'd run as if it were a game, but then my father's voice would call out to us to be careful. It was no game at all.

After five years of exhausting and painful cancer treatments that weakened our Dad, and unending checkups that we dreaded every time, my father came home one day from the Veteran's Administration Hospital and told us a story.

He said he had gone to the doctor's that day, and when he walked in there was a huge and heavy file on the doctor's desk. It was my father's medical chart. Volumes thick.

The doctor had smiled at him and said, "Mr. Young, I don't get to do this very often." He pulled a thick black marker from his lab coat pocket and wrote in large letters across the front of the file, "CURED!" He underlined it three times. The two men smiled.

My mother cried, and laughed, and hugged my father when

he told us. The aunts cried when my mother called them. I cried, not really understanding at seven years old what *cured*, meant: but maybe it meant my father wouldn't have to go away any more.

It was in the autumn of 1967, the same fall the Red Sox won the pennant. We loved that year.

But by the next February he was sick again. I remember the night. Particularly dark. Raining. Did it always rain the nights my father didn't come home? I remember my mother trying not to look scared in front of us. But we all knew, without saying a word, she was waiting for the phone to ring. For the news of what had happened to him.

Finally, a coworker of my father's called. Chest pain. They had rushed him to the hospital. The doctor would call as soon as he could.

Well-intentioned neighbors came to take us kids for pizza. They thought it would cheer us up. I remember sitting in the back seat of their car, crowded between my two brothers, feeling outraged that these people had taken me away. What if I was needed at home? What if there was news only I could handle?

When we got back, my mother was sitting alone in the living room. We sat with her as she stared out the window. Nobody turned the television on. We just waited. The rain turned into a blizzard that whitened the sky and filled the fields and roads with deep drifts of snow.

The doctor called. A large blood clot had formed and traveled into my father's lung. He was lucky to be alive. They would keep him in the hospital, on blood thinners, for at least a week.

Even if we had owned a car reliable enough for the two-hour drive to the hospital, my mother could not have gotten out that night. It was a huge storm. Two days before the plows could get to us.

. . .

My parents' best friends, Ding and Leanie Martin, came as
soon as they could make their way up the road. While Leanie
stayed with us kids, Ding drove my mother to the hospital.

And while we waited for my Dad to come back to us, my
brothers and I got up each day and ate our sugar cereal with an
extra spoonful of sugar on top. We went to school and tried to
apply ourselves to the magnitude of the multiplication tables,
or the urgency of knowing the names of all the capitals of the
United States. Then we came home and watched scratchy television cartoons while my mother put on her waitress uniform
and headed for work.

Then he came back again.

He played catch with Richie out by the pasture. And
coached Little League. He showed Peter how to tame a rac-
coon for a pet. And spent too much on a stereo system for Peter that had a wicked cool record player and speakers as big as
a bag of grain. He drove me all the way to the regional school,
four towns away, because I felt alone on the bus. He taught me
on those rides to love the music of Kris Kristofferson, Willie
Nelson, and Loretta Lynn. Sometimes he'd turn off the eight-
track tape and ask me to sing him a song.

But a few years later, more happened. The migraines started—
bad ones where he couldn't open his eyes or speak. My mother
would lie for hours, next to him on their bed, rubbing his neck,
behind his ears, his forehead. She would close the door so we
kids wouldn't worry, but I would stand there sometimes and listen, waiting, in case there was something I could do.

And then, a day later, maybe a few days, the headache would
release. He would come back to us. Really back. The vibrant
Dad.

He was a man who loved a hobby. He collected coins. He

searched out unusual antiques. He formed a barbershop quartet with old friends, and sang the national anthem with his whole chorus one glorious opening day for the Boston Red Sox at Fenway Park.

And he was such a good Dad. He let my brothers and me drive his car all over the farm, through the fields and around the apple trees, as soon as we were old enough to see over the steering wheel because he understood how good it is to take a road trip and he wanted us to know too.

But then he would get sick again. Doors would close. Trouble would hover. What could a five or seven or ten year old do?

I had trouble entrusting my family's security to the adults in my life. I was a strong little girl. Bossy. Sure things would go better if I could just pay enough attention.

It was a lot of work.

My mother would find me, sometimes in the middle of the night, at my desk, talking in my sleep. Muttering, working and working at some problem I imagined there. Mom would lead me back to bed, tuck me in, and tell me it was time to rest.

But how do you rest when you know trouble waits at the door?

Back when we burned down the fields, it took all afternoon and well into the night to get the job done. After many hours of our vigil, my mother would call in my brothers and me. Long past our bedtime. Come on in now, you kids. We stripped from our smoky layers of pants and shirts, and washed off in the old, iron tub. The blackened water swirling down the drain left peculiar patterns along the tub that disturbed me in a way I couldn't quite name.

I'd get into my bed, the smell and taste of smoke still filling my nose and mouth. I would lean toward my bedroom window to see my father, outlined in the night, far down the field. I'd watch as he'd light another cigarette, adding that tiny red glow to the snakes of embers that seemed to crawl alive along the burning fields.

My eyes would be heavy with sleep and smoke, and I would will myself to stay awake, to watch for that dangerous burst of flame that might slip past them, but not me.

A sudden small fire would flare up, and Dad and Bill would rush to stomp it back, their faces distorted by the light of flames at their feet. My heart clenched. Surely it would take all three of us to do the job.

The next morning, the sun on my bed was a surprise—I had slept. The night was over. The sound of my father and mother's voices and the smell of coffee from the kitchen were the reassurance I held my breath for. We had, for another night, averted danger in my family. For now, my watch was done.

# CHAPTER SEVEN

# The Further Complication

WE DIDN'T HAVE SO MANY photographs in the family where I grew up. Film cost too much and so did processing. Also, there was a particular organizational quality in remembering to take the pictures in the first place and then to have them developed—these were qualities we did not seem to have.

But other people took pictures and sometimes gave us copies. In one photograph, my brothers and I are in the backyard of our first house, right after my father's illnesses and the trouble with the church. Dad had it framed and kept it on his bureau for the rest of his life, a happy picture of us, the sister and her two brothers, together in the yard.

But now I study it as a piece of evidence. The hardest things you could imagine had happened to these three children, and yet there they are, together and smiling at their parents who stood just beyond the camera. It is not just a photograph. It is proof that we survived.

In the picture I'm in the middle—happiest always when I

am at the center of things—and my older brother, Peter, is leaning against me. Richie is holding his blanket and sucking his thumb, smiling a big wet smile.

I study the picture again and look at Peter. It occurs to me now that his pose is like pictures I've seen of sultry fifties movie stars like Jayne Mansfield. It reminds me how it confused me when he acted like a girl. I didn't understand why he wasn't like other boys or why it made the grownups even more uncomfortable than it did me.

My brother was an artistic boy. He drew amazing portraits of beautiful women in charcoal and pastels and hung them on the walls of his bedroom. He had the first pair of bell-bottoms in our town, when all of the other boys were wearing farm jeans and flannel shirts that smelled like truck oil and hay. He was a sophisticated reader and he moved gracefully, like a young deer, in a town where boys were not supposed to read or be graceful. His differences were not interesting to others. They were bad.

But I adored my older brother. He protected Richie and me fiercely, like we were his very own.

Once, I was suddenly awakened to sounds in rooms below. My mother was screaming at my father and crying as his booming voice thrummed through the walls. I lay awake, completely alone and afraid, wondering what it all might mean. And then my older brother crossed the cool linoleumed hall, a slender boy of nine in striped pajamas, carrying our sleeping baby brother from their room to mine so we could wait it out, safer always with each other.

How was it that this boy could be so strong to us and seem so weak to everyone else? I just couldn't understand why people didn't see him like I did.

What an awful thing to love someone like we loved our brother, and have that person be so unacceptable to others.

I remember the disapproving ones, the looks of other people's fathers. Somehow neighbors and uncles could always sniff out something funny in him. Something feminine. And then, there were the kids at school, always looking for perceived weakness—those boys who drove their fathers' trucks, wore big boots, and stood like old trees, weighted and solid and unmovable.

Once, my mother dropped us off for a swim at the beach over in Center Harbor. As we walked toward the water we saw older boys out on the raft, three of them, shoving at each other—all that fighting and pushing those kinds of boys do. I felt my brother hesitate. I wanted to say, "Let's go for an ice cream instead, I don't even feel like swimming," but to admit I noticed the trouble was not our way.

"Hey Fem," they called out.

"What are they saying?" I asked. I was slow, didn't get it at first. And he made it seem like it was okay, it was a fun name like, "Hey, Bud," or "Yo, Chief!" But the way they said it made it sound girly and dangerous. "Going ssw-iim-ming?" they called.

What did they see in him? How could they see it? But they always have. We could never hide that my brother was different.

When I was in second grade, he in fifth, we went to skate after school at Leavitt Park where the firemen had flooded a rink for all the kids. We sat on the burning cold ice to tie up our laces and right away three boys skated over to us and taunted him. "Hel-lo girls!"

And they started pushing at him and shoving and he didn't do anything. He laughed like in a way it was okay, really, it was. But I could see in his eyes what they did to him.

I jumped all three of them, me with one skate on, one off, stumbling but fierce; seven years old, and all of them fifth graders. I punched at their heads I couldn't reach, their puffy coats, the winter air, anything to make them go away.

Later, after supper that night, my parents sat us down. I got in trouble for fighting. That's not what girls do. And he got in trouble for not fighting.

They didn't know, my parents, it was not quite that simple. It was not just Leavitt Park. I would never stop stumbling, slipping on one skate, punching at heads I'd never reach and at winter air.

The cruelty never stops, you see. When you have a brother who is gay, you are never quite free of other people's opinions. You hear things said over and over that remind you how wrong it is to be gay. A line will be drawn between God's true people and them, the sorry homosexuals. And yet because I love someone, deeply, who is gay, the lines don't fall so easily for me.

How many times have I been shown that first chapter of Paul's letter to the Romans with its harsh warning about men who "likewise gave up natural relations with women and were consumed with passion for one another, committing shameless acts. . . ."

Paul writes about other forms of improper conduct: envy, murder, strife, gossiping, boasting. Being faithless, heartless, and ruthless. But I don't hear people worrying so much about envy and ruthlessness. I certainly don't see too much focus on being heartless. What I hear is repulsion for homosexuals. That's it.

Paul goes on to say, "Though they know God's decree that those who do such things deserve to die, they not only do them but approve those who practice them." Is the Bible saying my brother deserves to die?

Oh, Paul. To die? Is that really how you want me to read that? And do you mean just the homosexuals or do you mean the ruthless and heartless as well? What can I make of such passages? I, who was brought up in a world where people had bumper stickers that proclaimed, "The Bible says it. I believe it. That settles it." How do I reconcile myself to the words?

What do I do with every person who couldn't tolerate the femininity in the boy my brother was? Who can't tolerate the homosexuality in the man he is now? What do I do with every person who made him feel bad about himself, and consequently made me feel bad about myself because I was his sister, and I loved him, and I was not going to join them in their tirades against him.

That's the tricky thing. It isn't that you have this brother who is gay, who is separate from you. When you have a gay sibling, you can't get away from it. It's your identity too. You don't get the gift of easy truths. You get the complication of God's word speaking out about someone you love as much as you love yourself.

And it isn't just church people. You've also got all those neighbors and school parents and community leaders taking a stand. And then there's the daily newspaper. There are plenty of reminders there of what people do with homosexuals. Oh, Lord.

My brother formally announced his homosexuality to my family when he was in his twenties. It was not news that surprised any of us. When you grow up with a gay brother, you know it.

He had tried not to be gay. He really did. He tried girlfriends and I particularly remember that final one, the last summer he lived in New Hampshire. She was twenty-four, beautiful, intense, and adoring. She was sure she could make him straight. She gave it her best shot; they both did, all that summer. I think of her now as a round of antibiotics, ignorantly prescribed.

Peter told me recently about the best part of being with that girl. He said it was one night when they went to the movies. He asked me, "Do you know how great it is to put your arm around the person you are with in a dark movie theater, and they lean into you, all warm, and nobody looks at you—it's okay?"

People always ask me how my parents handled this business of my brother being gay. I guess it would have been easier if he weren't gay. Easier for him, certainly. And easier for them. But easier isn't always a choice.

So my parents nurtured what was best in each of us. They were very, very good at loving us that way. And though it was hard sometimes, that isn't so much what I remember now. I remember my mother, crazy, blind in love with each one of us. To her we are the most amazing and beautiful people who have ever lived. I remember my father walking into the local diner one morning, where practically the whole town had breakfast each day, with my brother and his friend who were looking unmistakably like a pair of gay boys. Dad ordered his usual cup of coffee and eggs, had a smoke, and laughed with his son and his son's friend, and if any of those local guys had a thing to say about it, they didn't say it then.

When Peter was coming into his adulthood and was still living in New Hampshire, Dad sat him down and talked about how hard his life would be in such a small town. He suggested he move to the city so he could be who he was without so many looks of disapproval. He wanted him to have the best life he could and there was no denying that would be tough in Moultonboro.

My parents were people who cherished each of their three children. And they taught us to hold onto each other, no matter what. We were well practiced in being kicked out. That vote of the covenant at First Church showed every one of us, all too clearly, what happens when you don't act the way other people expect.

So we had an unspoken rule we lived by in our house. Nobody gets kicked out for good. We all messed up plenty of times—but we held on.

Un-churched though we were, we took God seriously. And to us, our parents' love was the way we learned about God's.

Now I am a parent wanting to teach my daughters about God. And to do that well, I need to tell them the way their gay uncle has been treated and how that has shaped who I am as a person trying to be a Christian. I need to tell them what I know about trying to find God when so many others try to tell you there is only one way.

I teach them to seek God in His astounding and confusing limitlessness. Not the small, prescribed god of easy answers. The God who is greater than any question or contradiction that might come our way.

I take them into the woods and to the tops of mountains to amaze them with what the Creator has done. I try to show them I can't live without Jesus and the things he did while here among us. And that I love the church so much, even though it's a place whose people still hurt me and others I care about.

And I show them that I love my gay brother and I love my straight brother and that I do not want to judge anyone but myself.

Yes, I know, I know. The Bible calls us to judge. I've been told that for years. But I've also read the part about removing the log from my own eyes before I try to take the splinter from another's. And about loving others as ourselves. And the part that Jesus said is the most important thing we do: *love the Lord our God with all your heart and all your soul and all your might.*

. . .

It's a tricky business though, to quote from the Bible. "You can't just go pulling out scripture to suit your purposes"—that's what my father used to tell us. "You don't get to like some parts, not the rest."

But for me this has always meant living with the fact that when the lines get drawn, too often, I am on the other side. I'm the girl who was told, "Your mother is a bad woman." Or, more recently, "I would not want you to lead our Sunday school unless you sign this statement against homosexuality." It has been implied, over and over, "You aren't really one of us unless you use the same words we use to talk about God."

And what do I do with these stands that leave me out?

I get away from the crowd and try to be still and know God. I go back to the woods of my girlhood. I sit and stare at small, perfect ferns. Sometimes I sing. Or turn to words Jesus said when he was here among us. I read, "Come unto me, all you who labor, and I will give you rest." That's what Jesus said.

Rest for me, with all of the many complications I bring to the table. Rest for my gay brother and for my straight brother. Rest for my divorced friend, and your alcoholic son, and your cousin and neighbor with their messed up lives, and everyone you think is too liberal and everyone you find too legalistic— for everyone who is trying to find their way to rest. Jesus can lead us to it.

Thirty years after my family was kicked out of the church, my father died. He died of a sudden heart attack in the middle of the night. My mother felt him missing from the bed, found him on the bathroom floor, and called Richie who came right over to help. Then he called my house and Peter's to tell us to come on home.

I drove to the airport that morning as it was getting light.

Peter was on his way. I went alone so that I could cry as hard as I needed to, without my little daughters seeing how grief was clawing apart their mom.

I waited for his flight in an airport that was suddenly crowded, and then empty again. I leaned my body, heavy, against the window of a closed coffee shop. I couldn't seem to stop crying, but nobody came to help me. All those heaving sobs and not one person stopped to inquire.

I thought about the time when I was five years old, listening to my parents fight in rooms below. I thought about how alone I felt that night. And I remembered how Peter, that slender boy of nine in striped pajamas, snuck into my room with baby Richie asleep in his arms, because we were always safest with each other.

I heard a bell announcing his flight and stood up and wiped my face. I watched as the plane unloaded crowds of people into the hallway but none of them was the one I needed. I looked up and saw him, finally, more handsome and tall than the rest, walking way at the back, down the linoleum hall toward me.

We held each other and cried and then walked slowly to the car to begin the drive to our brother and our mother and our dead father and the place where we all used to live.

# CHAPTER EIGHT

# Jesus Hippies and Herbal Tea

IN THE EARLY SEVENTIES, when I was a teenager, I became involved with a youth group that was part of the growing Jesus Generation. My parents watched as I went off to meetings several times each week and came home singing Christian folk songs and praising God.

By that time we had sold off most of the animals on the farm, and kept just a couple of cows and the occasional pig. The intensity of my father's passion for the farm had waned. Both of my parents were working long hours at jobs they didn't love, trying to pay the bills. My older brother and I were in high school. Our little brother was occupied with the innocent world of Little League and playing with trucks. We all seemed to be going in different directions.

At the youth group meetings, I recaptured some of the good feelings I remembered and missed from church. There was singing and swaying, holding hands and praying and crying and loving. The meetings were held in a barn that belonged to a wonderful hippie couple we knew in town. We would all gather in our big, bulky sweaters and build a fire in the wood stove and begin our praise.

We would gather around a person and lay hands on them and call out our prayers to God. I remember the feeling of those hands on my head and shoulders and back. I remember the smells of everyone so close, the smells of wood stove smoke on wool, the smells of the herbal teas we sipped from hand-thrown mugs. I remember how good those hands felt, how good it was to be connected to church friends again.

With all the gladness I was feeling about being back at church, it made me wonder how my father could have left the joy he had felt as a brand-new minister. He was just starting his new career when they kicked us out. But it was like he had forgotten about all that now. I didn't understand how.

One night he came in to kiss me good night after I got home from a prayer and praise meeting. I asked him the question I had been thinking about for months, "How could you have just given up on God like you did?"

The Jesus hippies used to call those confrontations, *Truth in Love*. They were part of the hyper-honesty that we valued. The idea was that you could say whatever you wanted to say to a person as long as you intended it in love.

My father looked at me, perhaps a little sadly, perhaps knowingly—I couldn't quite read him. He started to reach for the packet of cigarettes in his shirt pocket. But then changed his mind. He looked at me. I remember his quiet answer, "Jesus Christ will never fail you. But people will fail you every day of your life." He shut the door softly as he left the room.

And they did fail me, my Jesus hippie friends. During the years I attended, there were power struggles among the elders of the group. One was sure God was calling him to be the leader. Another was sure it was meant to be him. God was saying this. God was certainly saying that. They were struggles that now seem so predictable, but back then felt so devastating.

There were so many who absolutely knew what God had to say and what he meant. They received more prophecies than Isaiah, and were not afraid to call them out, completely sure of what each word meant.

We held Sunday services in a large, round church with a loft ceiling that lifted in the middle to a peak pointing the way to heaven. We sang one chorus after another, becoming more and more entranced as the music moved from joyous and upbeat to quiet and sorrowful.

I remember one service in particular. Brother Harry slowly stood up from his seat near the front and steadied himself with his cane. "Thus says the Lord," he yelled out into the waning afternoon light. "I see a raven, a dark, dark raven. Circling among us. Circling, dark. Circling, low. There is a raven among us, here in this very room! It is looking for a place to land. Oh, my people, don't let it land."

We all had our eyes closed, having been successfully lulled by the music. But I looked around surreptitiously, experiencing a sudden fear of birds. I could not see it myself, but I could feel that Brother Harry was right. It was surely there in the room.

"It will land if you let it, my brothers and sisters. This black, black bird has found the one on whom to land. Circling. Dark. Circling. Low."

Well, I was terrified. There were about three hundred people in the sanctuary, all gathered in large rows of circles, and I knew that at any moment that huge, black bird was going to land on my shoulder and everyone would be able to see. I was the *only* one in the place it would pick. I knew it.

Having been kicked out before, I was ready to be kicked out again.

I wondered how the sharp, dry talons would feel on my shoulder. If its oily feathers would brush my face and if it would hurt. And how I would get home with a bird gripped to my shoulder. It would be the outward sign of my inward shortcomings. I'd never get rid of it. How would I explain?

I waited, looking around for its approach.

"Circling low. Circling, circling, my brothers and sisters," he moaned, sorrowful but sure that the one among us was about to be revealed.

I wondered: *Why do I keep trying? Why do I keep thinking I can find a way to fit in?* There always seemed to be something about me that didn't get things right. I was too religious for some. Too worldly for others. But I so wanted God with me. I wanted to find my way to Him. I had to. Somehow.

The music, slowly filling in the background, began to pick up again. I opened my eyes and saw that others had opened theirs also. What about the bird? Nowhere in sight. Had there been a prophetic misunderstanding? Had it left?

I couldn't believe it. I had gotten away with it.

With what, I wasn't quite sure. But I joined in on the praise songs and smiled at the people who smiled at me.

I lasted with the church another few months. Then someone had a prophecy that my boyfriend and I were not right for each other. He was the first boyfriend I had had in years. One I really needed. The prophecy said I was too outgoing. God wanted a quieter girl for this young man. This was God's message to the elder's wife. Which she, of course, felt compelled to share. God had told her quite clearly, she assured me, that it was her niece, not me, who would be best for that young man.

It was almost laughable.

*Enough, already. Enough.* As much as I wanted God, I was sick to death of His people. Of their incessant manipulations.

I thought of my father's words that people would fail me every day of my life. I was starting to understand. I looked across the table at the elder's wife with her expression so earnest, stood from the table, and left the room.

# CHAPTER NINE

# Swimming in New Places

WHEN I WAS A GIRL, my brothers and cousins and I swam as much as we could. We swam in the brook on our farm, we swam down at Ding and Leanie Martin's pond, and especially, we swam in Lake Winnipesaukee. We loved the big lake.

Though *we* were not lake people. Lake people stepped outside the doors of their well-appointed cottages and swam in the deepest, clearest water. They ran to lovely lakefront homes for refreshing cold lunches or quick naps.

We townspeople swam down at the public access. Parked our hot cars alongside boat trailers and portable bathrooms. Carried paper bags of towels, cheap sunscreen, thin lemonade, chips, and tuna sandwiches (which would all too soon become sandy and warm). The packed ground and asphalt from car to beach burned our feet.

But we swam anyway. Most every day in the summer. My mother sat on her frayed towel and talked for hours with my Aunt Elinor. They never minded taking us to the beach, staying as long as we wanted and watching while we yelled, "Look, Mommy! Watch this one!" They took a few quick dips themselves during the day, though my mother wouldn't get her hair wet because she had to go to work later. She and my aunt would stand and talk in the water (they always had more to say), and spread their legs wide as they stood there, so we kids could swim through their legs. Finally, when we tired of the game, they would go back to their towels for a paper cup of lemonade. And we would swim back out to the raft where they watched all of our dives and flips, as if they really *were* incredibly interesting.

Then when Peter got his license, he became the family explorer of new waters. He found The Pothole, that gloriously cold spot on the river with glacier-carved pockets of bedrock so deep you could disappear into them.

He found Beede Falls, which became our family's favorite spot for a supper picnic. He found it because he liked to drive on roads he didn't know and see where they might take him. Peter had my father's sense of adventure. Of trying new things.

He went driving up into Sandwich Notch, where the deep-rutted road was so narrow, if another car came along you had to back up and pull over in the fern-covered woods.

There he found the enormous rock and waterfall. Biggest rock we'd ever seen. Any of us. And then he followed the river that flowed from the falls, even deeper through green woods. The green woods that became more brilliant the farther in you went, to a favorite spot we might never have known, if not for my brother's wandering ways. There was a long, slippery rock where he took us to slide, in old jean shorts, into a startling clear basin of cold river water.

Peter taught us there were beautiful places other than the farm.

He taught me about art as well. It was this whole other world beyond the brooks and lakes, a world in which I also learned to swim.

When I was sixteen Peter, our cousin Laurel, and I took the train to the Museum of Fine Arts in Boston. I remember standing in front of the sculpture, *The Dancer*, by Degas. I stared at the young ballerina's pose: her strong legs, her arms pulled behind her back, the confidence of her jutting chin. Something happened to me when I saw her. It was partly the way Degas had loved what he saw in that dancer. Something I saw too. It was partly the way it seemed she had always existed and he just brought her to be. And it was also the way she looked so brave to me. Young and brave. That's what I thought when I looked at her. Because she wasn't perfectly smooth and proportioned like other artists' renderings of ballerinas I saw that day. There was a coarseness to her. Like maybe she was from a small town, too.

I began to skip school to go look at art. My Dad would glance at the odometer in the car he let me use and say, "Wow, that trip to high school gets longer every day." And I would smile at him, charm him. And explain how I *couldn't* go to school every day. There were other things I needed to see.

He told me he used to skip a lot of school too. He would wave to his mother and begin the walk to high school. Then, when he was out of her view, he'd stick out his thumb and hitchhike up to Maine where he boarded his horse, Tony. My dad, at sixteen, would ride that horse bareback all day long, and then thumb a ride back to the city, home in time for dinner.

When I graduated, I was voted most independent in my senior class. My Dad was more excited than if I had been voted most likely to succeed. He told me, with great pride, that he had been voted most independent too. He had great hopes for me.

I went to a state college nearby and studied English. A restlessness had formed in me for all the new worlds and ideas I was starting to see beyond the comforting acres of our farm. I wanted to be a part of everything that was new to me. I was ready. But not completely.

I went home to my parents' farm almost every weekend. It was like our after supper games of hide-and-seek in the near dark when I was a little girl. I loved the thrill of seeing how far away I could run and hide. But I would crouch in my hiding spot behind the barn, under the wheelbarrow, longing for that moment when one of my brothers would call, "All-y, all-y, all come free!" and I could dash to the one big rock we called *gools*. Home. Safe.

My parents were beginning to talk about selling the farm. I didn't want to have to stay there, but I wanted *them* to. That was when I started to write poems. Poems about the farm. About leaving places.

And I read. Constantly. Emily Dickinson, who was so much a part of the world and yet so disconnected, too. I knew her. And Henry David Thoreau, who could stare at a pond even longer than I could.

I spent four years studying the ways writers find words for experience. Then it was time to leave that place too. I didn't want to go. I had belonged in those classroom discussions and in the crammed offices of my English professors I frequently visited in a way I had never belonged before. But my four years were up.

When I graduated from college, my parents gave me the money for a summer trip to Europe. A gift I still marvel at: it wasn't the kind of experience we were used to thinking we could have in our family.

But my cousins Cheryl and Laurel were going. I wanted, desperately, to go as well.

The trip was a package deal for college graduates. Four Volkswagen vans. Two months of reservations at youth hostels and campgrounds from Belgium to Italy and all around in between.

My Dad worked it out so that I could fly to Boston with a rich guy in town who owned his own plane. I had one small bag crammed with clothes and journals. My camera. Good sneakers. My mother was sure she would never see me again.

I had never been on an airplane. Neither had either of my parents. I had never been out of New England.

And in three days I would be in London. In two weeks, Paris. I would see museums *full* of Degas statues. I used to stare at pictures of the Swiss Alps and the winding streets of German towns in the stacks of Tessie and Dick Wakefield's *National Geographic* magazines. But now I, a girl from Moultonboro, would step right into those bright and shiny pages, touch the snow, and smile at the round-faced woman with the armful of crusty bread. Me.

When we got to the field that was our town's airport, I turned to my Dad. "I'm so scared," I told him.

"Oh, Hon, but this is a great thing," he said. "My daughter. A college graduate. Europe. You're gonna see it all."

The man with the airplane was already in the cockpit adjusting buttons and knobs. My Dad threw my bag behind the seat and helped me climb in. It all happened so fast I barely had time for a last hug.

But I looked down as we flew away and saw my Dad, Dick Young, standing there in the airport field by Berry Pond. He wore his usual loose jeans. It was hot enough that he had switched his flannel shirt for plaid short sleeves, permanent press. His arms were tan from the elbow down.

He was reaching up into the air, giving me the thumbs-up: his enthusiasm, utter joy. He was waving that thumbs-up victory sign to me as though he was throwing a baseball up into the air over and over, yet standing far below, his feet firmly planted on the ground of my hometown.

The airplane lifted higher and soon all I could see was the outline of the town field behind us. But I knew he was still there, watching me go. *Go, go. Live this life, Kate Young. And love it.*

It was several weeks already into the trip. Laurel and I had tasted pints of bitter in British pubs, stood this close to Michelangelo's *David.* Walked along the D-Day beaches. Stood in the showers of Dachau. Climbed hills and picked wildflowers in Switzerland. Drunk thick coffee at little tables in little towns all across France.

Europe was so different. And, too, it was like a thousand hometowns crowded together. Some of them were like mine. And some of them weren't. But they were all hometowns to somebody. Places where people lived and worked and swam. Just like us.

The best swimming was in Greece. Our group had arrived at a campground late the night before, grimy with travel, and achy from all the lumpy belongings jammed against us in the hot van. We were too tired to set up tents, so slept beneath the stars near the briny water we could not see, but could hear and breathe in.

The ground beneath my sleeping bag that night was particularly hard. Finally, gratefully, it was morning. Just barely. I whispered to Laurel, "Do you want to swim?"

We left the circle of sleeping bags, the crowd of tired travelers, curved into and around each other: a crumpled alphabet of brightly colored covers and snoring bodies.

We left them and walked to a long, low bathhouse where we stripped off our sweaty clothes and pulled on thin, smooth bathing suits. Our bodies were younger then. Our thighs not yet padded with pregnancies; our breasts still high and un-tugged by greedy baby mouths.

The water was cool in the just-dawn air. We were buoyed by the water's saltiness in this surprising way we had not known back at our lake in New Hampshire. We were swimming in Greece, and it was the same and it was different. We laughed at our good fortune, turned somersaults, bared our breasts and bottoms, holding our suits in a fisted grip, ready to pull them back on if anyone came by—just like we did at home, late at night, worried a police car might pull up when we went for midnight swims after our waitress shifts.

Now, here in Greece, we spit salty saliva from our mouths and laughed at our pleasure, and laughed at our laughter, and the way it carried across the sea and nearly roused the sleeping forms in their crumpled state.

Farther down the beach a group of nuns approached us, their black robes dragging in the sand, brushing a curving trail behind them. We kicked our legs and pressed our arms through the water, floating so easily in the salty buoyancy, watching the heavily robed women with their roped waists and covered heads.

I was aware of the many layers covering their bodies and of our own nakedness, as if the Sisters could see through the swells of the Aegean Sea's bright green-blue teal to our forgot-ten modesty. As if they would mind. Terribly.

But as I watched them I could see that they were not even aware of us.

They were all talking at once, these nuns, and walking, pulling along the sand like great, heaving birds.

They laughed, suddenly. Laughed heartily, you could even say. Like my mother and Leanie walking down the path to Ding and Leanie's pond. Or Mom and my Aunt Elinor, laughing as they sat for hours on beach towels at the lake. Or like any women, anywhere, laughing because they are together and it is morning and it makes a person glad to be near water.

And the many tones and pitches of the nuns' laughter cut through the layers of my understanding of who they were: Covered. Cloistered. Limited in ways I was sure I never would be.

I, twenty-one years old, swam with my cousin, the companion of my childhood—thinking I had life figured out. That it was as simple as whether you swam naked or walked, uniformed, along the shore.

We, who were about to return to the States and say yes to the marriage proposals that would come to each of us within months of our return. As if we knew, too, what that might mean.

As if it were a simple thing—this knowing how to choose to live. Whether you spent your days in New Hampshire or in Greece. Covered or uncovered. As if there were such a thing as one best way.

# CHAPTER TEN

*Found*

THE MONTHS I SPENT TRAVELING in Europe marked the passage between the years of my childhood in New Hampshire, and the years of my marriage and motherhood in the city.

When the airplane that brought me home landed in Boston, Roy Caley's face was the first I saw. I could feel his joy reaching toward me all the way through the heavy doors of customs, which opened and closed with a maddening and slow repetition. I could see him. Then not see. I pushed my way forward, impatiently, trying to get through the crowds of people and backpacks and heavy suitcases. Trying to get to him.

My parents were there as well: my mother crying at the miracle that I had survived a foreign land, and my father smiling, perhaps shyly, as he looked between Roy and me, his only daughter. I think even then we all knew that I was not coming home to them. I was ready to move from New Hampshire, at twenty-one, to start my life with that young man whose smile was so kind I was willing to trade being among my mountains and woods each day just to be near the hope that smile gave me.

I knew I could join my life with his because he loved the farm where I grew up almost as much as I did. He loved New Hampshire, my parents, and my brothers. And he understood that although I was excited to move to the city, I would never, truly, leave that life.

But I did move. Because I trusted him. Because of the ways he made me laugh, his able appreciation for things beautiful to the eye, and, especially, his desire to be near to God.

The ways I felt when I was with Roy were worth the trade of my familiar hometown for the unfamiliar ways of the city where we bought our first home.

The neighborhood where we lived was so packed with buildings and noises I didn't know if I could ever get used to it. But I loved being a subway stop from the museums; the movie theaters, music and restaurants of Harvard Square; and all the different kinds of people (sometimes missing my stop on the train because I was so busy *looking*).

The houses on our street, separated only by the thin strips of concrete that served as driveways, were so close I could hear my neighbor rinse herself as she lingered in her nightly bath. I could also hear, too easily, too often, the anger from the family on the second floor. The continual insults.

But we wanted an old house in an old Boston neighborhood. While our friends were looking to buy brand-new houses in the suburbs, we loved what was old.

The house we bought was in a long row of three-deckers, one like the next: three floors of apartments stacked one on top of the other, with porches front and back. It had been constructed beautifully, solidly. The intricacies of the detail with which they had been built—heavy, ornamental molding, beveled and leaded glass on even the most common windows, oak doors that weighed a hundred pounds each, and high, high ceilings—appealed to our hungry senses.

They were places with character that had been lived in for a hundred years by people we never knew. Nameless other couples, starting out like us. The new brides kept their best dishes in the built-in dining room cupboard behind this same thin and polished glass as I did.

We stripped walls of the crumbling paper they had chosen and washed off layers of old glue. I got a black marker and we each signed our names in the corner of the dining room wall before repapering. We stood back and smiled and then I added, in big letters, "I love Roy Caley, that's why I live here. 1982."

We sanded floors and painted ceilings so high our arms ached for days from the long reach. We collected furniture at yard sales and from my parents' house and from Roy's favorite great-aunt. We ate a lot of boxed macaroni, and that first winter before we got the furnace working, our apartment was always cold. At night, before bed, we would sometimes drive over to Linda Mae's Restaurant and order a basket of rolls, the cheapest thing on the menu. We stretched out our cups of coffee to soak up all the warmth we could before heading back.

And although we were aware that some of our friends thought we were crazy, we would say to each other, "Someday we're going to miss all this." Because we loved what we were trying to find together.

We spent hours walking though the neighborhoods that surrounded our street. And for every sight that made me sad, we would find something beautiful.

There was our favorite garden, tended to by a bent-over old woman, always in a cardigan, whom we came to call Miss Glory. She earned this name for having the most magnificent mass of morning glories either of us had ever seen. Not a string or two, dotted here or there with a flower: but a jungle of morning glories, each blossom bluer and more perfect than the next. Miss Glory's flowers spread all the way from the front to the back of her enormous yard. On particularly noisy days, we would walk the three blocks to her house, just to be quieted by the beauty we found there.

On our walks we discovered a circle of Victorian houses lit by original gas lamps; a golden stained glass window that lit up in the afternoon light like a church; a house with a hidden side porch, which we coveted for its mass of dense trees; and the place across the street from it with Mabel, the friendliest dog for miles around.

We found each beautiful object and place available to rest our eyes from what was hard about city living. And then we began to work to make a garden refuge of our own.

Our yard was about the size of two station wagons parked next to each other. That's what most of the other yards had in them: old cars. But Roy and I shared a love of gardening, so our first summer together we cleared out the thick weeds that persisted amidst empty whiskey nips, rusty spark plugs, and broken-down chairs that people threw off their porches rather than carry to the street on trash day. We dug in peat and manure and clean soil.

Our first garden had enough basil to keep us in pesto sauce and basil and tomato sandwiches for months. We also planted zinnias and cosmos: bright flowers that drew our eye from chain-link fences and the fume-y gas station two doors down.

Evenings after work, we sat at a French table and chair set (a wedding gift and the nicest thing we owned) on our back porch and lit candles and drank wine. There were many long hours of uninterrupted conversation in those early years of our marriage. We loved that back porch and its view of thirty or so other back porches, like stage sets with their own little dramas.

Each night, we looked up to see if the grandmother a few

houses away was out for her evening ritual of drying her long, thick hair. As she ran her brown hands through the tangles that hung from her head in gleaming curls, she smoked a thick cigar and blew long streams of smoke high into the air. She would turn her head sometimes and look right at me and laugh. I think that she could see that she scared me a little. I felt as young and out of place as she knew I was.

On another porch a young man with a tiny waist danced to his newest record glaring from a small player. Little kids rode plastic tricycles on some of the porches, and banged into each other and cried. And some of the porches were always empty—as if the people crowded inside had no need for the coolness of evening air.

Our porch, overlooking our tiny garden and the porches of so many other lives, was the place where we began to define who we were and who we wanted to become in this life. It was the place where I wrote my first story. The place where Roy told me his goals, showing me how he was going to get to them. It was the place where, in a few years to come, we would tell my cousin Laurel and her husband Cal that Roy and I were having a baby.

And it was on this porch that we talked for hours about what we longed for in a church. A church that, like our house and neighborhood, was old and beautiful and diverse.

We attended the Presbyterian Church where Roy had grown up and where we had been married. And though our many connections to the place were important to us, we knew that we were looking for something more.

He needed to be free of everyone seeing him as someone's child or sibling. I needed to be appreciated as someone other than his wife. And we needed a place where we could define and redefine who we were and who God was to us—not a place where our beliefs were already presumed and defined and cast. We were a young couple looking to find out about God, together, in new ways.

The long avenue that ran through the center of the streets of our neighborhood was crowded, as always, with people hurrying down the sidewalks looking angry or lazing in doorways as though they planned never to get up again. It was jammed with run-down businesses, too many stoplights, and children running barefoot and shirtless, drinking sugary drinks from sticky bottles.

We were stopped at a red light when we saw a man dressed in a full-length cassock, all black, buttoned with one hundred buttons—from the street where his hem brushed scraps of lottery tickets—right up to his throat and the tiny white square of his religious calling.

The paradox of this man, walking slowly with his hands behind his back and the ease with which he made his way down the deteriorating avenue, caused us to slow the car to see where he might go. The way he seemed to float in that full-length cassock above the swarm of the city was something I needed to understand.

He crossed the avenue, not waiting for the pedestrian light. We turned down the street where he was heading, feeling an unspoken urge to follow him. Pulling our car off to the side of the street, we watched as the man climbed the steps of an enormous Gothic Revival structure. It loomed right there beside the crowded, all-night convenience store and the subway station to downtown Boston.

As large as the church was, it had a quiet presence—imposing and yet unimposing—it was a strong and tall old woman not heeding the change and confusion and noise around her.

Still following, and unsure of what we might find, Roy and I pulled into the parking lot of the church. A sign near the door read, "The Parish of All Saints, Ashmont. The Episcopal Church Welcomes You. Holy Eucharist Weekdays at 7:00. Solemn High Mass Sundays at 10:00."

I had never heard the word *Eucharist*. Was unsure just what an Episcopalian stood for. But we stared at the complication of vines on stonework. Wondered for how many years the gnarled canes of roses had grown there at the base of a castle-like tower that jutted up into the sky from the main building of the church. Unlike the wooden churches of my youth, this one made me think of cathedrals I had seen in England. Right here in our very own neighborhood.

Just then the vesper bells began to ring, a clear call above the city noises.

Vesper bells and sirens. Vesper bells and the honking of an angry horn. Vesper bells and a shouting fight erupting between two men on a porch across the street.

I listened to the deep call of the bells. Roy and I looked at each other without speaking.

The next Sunday, we attended.

Walking toward the entrance of the church, practically right on the busy street, we saw enormous, granite steps. There was comfort for me in that familiar, New Hampshire rock. Roy held open the front doors to me, but instead of stepping into the church as we expected, we found ourselves in a little outer room: an enclosed porch. Placed on a table against the wall was a vase jumbled with black-eyed Susans and Queen Anne's lace, flowers I would pick in the fields at the farm. But these were gathered, I would later learn, by one of the old ladies of the guild, from the edges of the subway tracks behind the church.

We stepped up to the thick dark wood of the main doors and peered through the tiny leaded glass windows into the enormous sanctuary. Heaving the giant doors open (not an easy pull), we stepped inside. "Wow," Roy whispered and took my hand.

It took a few moments for our eyes to adjust. No hanging fluorescent lights revealed all there was to see with a single sweep of an eye. The space was silent. All was dim and still.

Almost a city block away, it seemed, was an altar. Everything in the church summoned us closer toward it. We walked the long line of the main aisle, passing row after row of heavy, dark pews—straighter and taller than the ones we were accustomed to.

We had arrived early, and now took our time as we looked at the matching side aisles and stained glass windows of long-gone men and women, holding staffs and jugs and babies, as if yearning to tell us their stories.

We passed wrought iron stands of lighted candles, dripping wax down their long tapers. Roy pointed to a worn tapestry shield hanging from a stand: a small kingdom radiated with the shining sun embroidered above it. It was like the protected kingdom we were trying to find for ourselves. I smiled and squeezed his hand.

Drawing as near to the front as we could without calling attention to ourselves, we found our way to a straight-backed pew and sat down. Though I found it bare and uncomfortable, strict compared to the cushioned seats of churches we knew, I was grateful for what appeared to be foot rests at our feet. Nice touch, I thought.

From this closer view, I noticed the altar was lined with candles almost as tall as me. How did they light those things? Ladders? A single cross, perfectly polished, absorbed the morning light from high upper windows shining down as if with this single illuminating purpose. Beneath the cross was a gleaming brass door affixed to a little stone box. And when I strained my eyes to focus, I saw it had a tiny key in its little lock.

All of these enormous arches, the exaggerated length of
lines, patterns of light and color, dark corners of shadow, and
small glow of candle—all of it led to a little locked door.

There were some people already sitting around us. A few
more came quietly in. No one spoke to the others or called
across the space or waved. They bowed down on one knee,
slowly, all the way to the floor before entering their pews. Even
the surprisingly large number of elderly men and women knelt
with a slow, intentional motion that must have strained their old
knees.

A bell rang and everyone stood, so we did too.

The organ sounded, startling in the way it echoed in the
vastness, and Roy and I searched among the various volumes
in the pew rack for the hymnal. We found the right page about
halfway through the second refrain.

We watched as a parade of choirboys walked slowly in,
holding their music stiffly in front of themselves. It was all so
incredibly formal and yet these boys (from the baby-faced, five
year olds to the dyed-haired teenagers) were clearly at ease in
their choir cassocks and the starched fans of Elizabethan col-
lars rubbing at their throats. They processed in, smallest to tallest, and their voices were so high and sweet I closed my eyes
and listened, not wanting anything to distract me from the
pure sounds.

The procession continued with three men. The one in the
center carried a high cross. As it was carried past, everyone
around us bowed (and we, too late, bowed as well). The two
men on either side of the cross carried swinging canisters
smoking with incense. They waved them at us on long lengths
of chain. People bowed again.

Behind them, finally, slowly, came priests in heavy brocade
robes, layers and layers of complicated fabric on this warm July

morning. They, too, walked intentionally, their hands folded, and held just below their hearts, in prayer.

We, the congregation, watched. No one spoke. No one moved. No one hurried.

Roy and I stood and took in the inefficiency of this arrival. I did not know what he was thinking, though I wanted to ask. But this didn't seem to be a talking church. In the church we had been attending, I would have put my arm around him and said anything I wanted. Here instead, I stood quietly, waiting for what would happen next.

The priests processed beyond the congregation, beyond the choir, up a series of narrow steps to the altar. They bowed and then turned to us.

One offered the opening refrain. But instead of reading it off quickly, he lifted his arms, weighted by those brocade layers, and chanted familiar words in an unfamiliar way, *Hear what the Lord, God, says. Thou shalt love the Lord thy God with all thy heart and with all thy soul and with all thy might. This is the first and great commandment and the second is like unto it. Thou shalt love thy neighbor as thyself. On these two commandments hang all the law and prophets.*

Coming from the traditions of Protestant and Evangelical churches, this chanting was a little frightening. *Chanting?* The only people I had ever seen chant were peculiar cult members who hung out at Boston Common. The words were straight from the Bible—at least we could relax about that, but there *was* the incense issue. What do we think about incense? And those burning brass lamps hanging from the ceiling. Was this a Catholic church? Because that was *definitely* a statue of Mary in the corner.

Hmmm. This might take some explaining.

The service proceeded through seemingly random moments of standing and bowing, sitting and standing, listening to long passages of Scripture, and singing discordant notes that sounded austere to my gospel-hymn-loving ears.

We tried to negotiate our way through the pile of books that everyone else seemed to manage so nicely. "You handle the hymnal," Roy said finally, "and I'll do this one," referring to a red volume with the words *Book of Common Prayer* inscribed across the front.

We tripped through our first Sunday at All Saints, confused but *drawn*.

Though the walls were cracked and the paint was peeling (and they would definitely need to address the moisture issue soon), we found a deep beauty in our surroundings and in the service that day that compelled us.

As the priests prepared the Eucharist, we watched closely, thinking of the contrast of our own tradition of little plastic cups filled with grape juice. Of square cubes of white bread that turned into an unfortunate goo when pressed to the roof of your mouth.

We watched—instead of the pre-prepared convenience of the monthly Lord's Supper—the slow, methodical washing of a brass cup and plate. We would wait and follow the careful preparations as a group, adding a bit of bowing here, a bit of censing there. Bells. More reciting of prayers.

And then the priest approached the little locked door. Carefully, intentionally, with his assistants at his side, he unlocked the shining door. I could not see what he removed but they all bowed, low, before it.

And then they led us in prayer: *We are not worthy so much as to gather up the crumbs under Thy table, but thou art the same Lord whose property it is to always have mercy.* There was something in those words, in the humbleness they evoked, that caused Roy and me to look at each other, surprised by the heat of tears in our eyes.

In the tradition we came from, Communion was our monthly right. We did not think of it as a gift. As sustenance that might change us if we let it. Or if we did, we were so rushed that we only had about three seconds to take it in before the ushers came looking for those tiny plastic cups.

We hesitated about taking our place in the line of people who walked to the altar. We did not know how to receive the Eucharist at an altar, but we did what we had done all morning: we imitated, trying on those words and movements that fit us unexpectedly well.

We were not sure what would happen at that altar rail, but we knew we were welcome there. The Eucharist was freely offered: no one told us not to come. *All* of us were worthy and unworthy at the same time. Come anyway.

The moment was one we had been building toward all morning and not to receive it was impossible. It was intended.

As we walked forward we looked at the people around us. Such an eccentric mixture of characters. We did not know anything about the Episcopal Church. We did not know that it tended to be well-to-do. Here, in our neighborhood, this was not the case. The congregation was like the city around us: some of everything.

There were rough-handed guys who might fit more appropriately at the bar across the street than here where the voices of little boys sang poems of mercy. There was a stately and perfectly coiffed woman dressed in her prim Chanel suit and coordinating hat (whom I would later come to recognize as the quintessential, stately Episcopalian), kneeling beside a fragile Vietnamese man in a torn shirt with pants cinched at his tiny waist.

Young West Indian women were leading old West Indian women. And there were people who looked professorial, and people who maybe hadn't finished high school. All of them—all of us—approached the altar. The bread and wine. We each took our turn kneeling before grace.

"Take, eat." That's what the priest said as he moved his hand in the sign of the cross and laid a round wafer into my palm and into the palm of my husband. We lifted the wafer to our lips as we had seen the people before us do. I began to chew mine up and then worried when I looked down the line and saw that no one else was chewing. I stopped. Had they swallowed it whole? How?

Then another priest approached slowly with the brass goblet, his wrist draped with an embroidered white cloth with which he wiped the rim after each sip. I saw the metal touch my husband's lips. The slow intimacy of this shared holiness.

I remember the goodness of the wine that first morning. The surprise of its complicated texture. My gratefulness for the way it melted the half-chewed wafer still in my mouth. The warmth in my throat, and the light stirring in my head as I swallowed the elements the people of this church called gifts.

We stood up from the rail and walked back down the long aisle to our seats. I saw people deep in prayer; bended at the knee on what were not foot rests after all, but kneelers. Lumpy, hard kneelers.

I knelt, too, and tried to be quiet, tried to find words for the experience, the minutes and motions of these acts. Roy and I knelt together, our shoulders touching, each considering the reasons why we might feel like we had come home.

We carried the smoke of incense in our hair and in our clothes. It lingered on us, long after we had gotten home. We sat on our back porch for hours talking about what had just happened to us.

That first Sunday morning at All Saints we found our church home. That's what we knew. The spiritual truths offered through the liturgy would keep us safe, even when the hardest things happened.

And though we continued to fumble with various Episcopalian intricacies the first several months we attended, we knew we belonged. All we needed to do was to enter in: let ourselves be carried closer to God on the words and ways that had carried searching people through centuries.

Be still. Watch and wait. Taste and see that the Lord is good.

Each week Roy and I return, to try to take a step closer to who God is and who God wants us to be. We return to the sameness of liturgy and present our lives and our hearts, which do not stay the same. We bring who we are that particular day. And have learned together to find mercy in the ritual and wonder we encounter.

And then, thank you God, we have brought our daughters as they were born to us. From the time they were just days old, they have been with us at the altar, beginning their way among the mysteries to be found there.

Now, we all have come to know the ancient motions and words as if they were our own breathing in and out. My husband, my daughters, and me. We bow and stand and bend and pray. And have through all the weeks of all these many years.

# CHAPTER ELEVEN

# The Last Day

THE NIGHT MY FATHER DIED, my cousin, Laurel, and I had spent the day skiing in northern New Hampshire. It was the day before my birthday. My present from Roy was a pair of lift tickets for me and my favorite cousin. It meant a couple of days away from our husbands and kids.

It had been too long since Laurel and I had been on an adventure together. We, who had loved to sleep under the stars beside Beede Falls, who drove Volkswagen vans across the crazy roads of Europe, whose favorite swims were the ones late at night with only the bright moon and the cool lake touching us. We, who had lived in a tent one summer, out in a field, and waitressed at the Hi-There Café, and hiked a different mountain every week.

But it had been years since we had such adventures. Too many years. Now we were women, quietly married. Now we were moms of little ones who needed us all day long, and then even from their sleep—they called for us.

But for this one day we were released. We were *us* again. Bold. Laughing at how we could untangle from responsibility and reclaim this lighter way.

We skied for hours, uninterrupted, unconcerned with duty. We took colorful pictures of ourselves lifting our poles in triumph, tossing our heads back in laughter, because we needed the proof that we could have adventure again.

On our way back home, we stopped at a favorite restaurant we hadn't been to in years. We each ordered a glass of wine, and let the warmth of it, and the wood stove nearby, melt into our worn-out bodies.

We had the kind of talk two women can only experience who have known each other their entire lives. About growing up together, and the aunts and uncles, and all the family stories—funny and sad—we remembered most. We talked about times we spent exploring the city where she lived, and days we spent at the farm where I lived, and that important combination of people and places in our lives.

We began to talk about how my father encouraged our early adventures. She remembered the way he let us drive the snowmobile late at night, when we were only ten years old, all through the snowy woods, far from the lights of the house.

I remembered the year he trained the crows, but it was a story that somehow Laurel had never heard. One spring, I told her, my father raised three crows from babies. He heard about them on "Swap-Shop," that scratchy radio source of so many of his good deals.

Each day when he went to work, driving around the state as a tax appraiser, he took the baby crows with him because they were too little to be left alone. He kept them in a metal cage that took up most of the front seat of his car, and as he drove, he reached in between the metal grids and patted their glossy wings and backs.

He had bought them when they were still babies, only a few weeks hatched. The first thing he did was to take each bird, one at a time, in his large hand and feed it canned dog food. He did this by scooping a finger full and shoving it down their thin throats. And every time he did it, he said, "Hello, crow. Hello, crow," teaching them, eventually, to come to the sound of his voice.

Then one day, a few months later, he announced they were ready to be let go. My Dad was certain, even though my brothers and I were not so sure, that they would come back. He lifted the cage from his car, and carried it down the lane by the biggest tree. He lifted each bird into the air and smiled as they flew off.

Laurel and I smiled at this picture of him because we could both, so easily, imagine him standing by the pine, one of his worn flannel shirts tucked into loose jeans, and a can of dog food in one hand, a finger of the mushy stuff held high in the air, calling, "Hello, crow. Hello, crow."

I took another sip of wine and told Laurel how they really did come flying back, just like he'd said, down from high branches where I hadn't seen them. How they had seemed to just disappear someplace high, beyond my sight. And then reappear from nowhere I could locate. How that scared me a little.

They would land on his shoulder and let him stick his finger, hunked with food, down their eager throats. They choked and cawed and stretched their large beaks for more. He wasn't scared at all.

And it was such Dick Young magic, how he made that happen.

Laurel and I shared a chocolate dessert to finish off our perfect time together: outdoors all day in the winter mountains, singing familiar songs on the drive, a wood fire, warm wine, comfort food. Old stories. We were getting drowsy. It was time to head back.

I told her that when my parents had heard about our ski plans, they had worried we would be too tired to drive back to Boston. They had invited us to stay the night with them, just a half hour away. We smiled about the way we were still girls to them, needing to be taken care of. But we decided we wanted the day completely to ourselves. We didn't want to be daughters or nieces or anything but free.

So we had one last bite of dessert, a sip of coffee, and then reluctantly left. Our time was up. It was time to turn into wives again. Into moms.

When we got to Laurel's house a couple of hours later, I called Roy to check in on everything at home. He told me that our two year old, Jennie, was sick with a croupy cough.

That old feeling—trouble when I was not paying attention—sluiced through my body.

He assured me it was okay. Have my time away, he said. Get some sleep. No doubt, I'd have my turn with Jennie and her croup the next night. And besides, it was my birthday.

He was right. I didn't have to feel guilty. So I hung up the phone, gave Laurel a goodnight kiss and climbed the stairs to bed.

The crescent moon rising coursed my bed with its clear, white light. The sheets were cold and I kicked my legs around to warm the bed. I had it all to myself. No little ones would wake me, wanting to crowd the warm place between their Dad and me. I took all four pillows for myself and curled up in the pile of blankets and fell deeply asleep.

I didn't hear the phone ring.

Laurel heard it. She heard it immediately and reached for it as if she could stop the danger of it from entering our night. She heard my husband's voice, his words, let out a sob, and then she went to climb the stairs to where I was.

She climbed them slowly, her strong legs suddenly weak. She stood, frozen for a few seconds, at the foot of my bed, and watched my peaceful sleep, me, not yet knowing my life was changed.

And she gave me all she could, I suppose—a few more moments, with a crescent moon looking on.

When her voice found its way through the moon, the layers of blankets and pillows, the snowy mountains and snowy trees and snowy trails that floated in my sleep, I turned to her.

"It's Roy," she said, "he's on the phone." Later I would remember that there was an absolute flatness to her voice, as if she were unwilling to commit to being any part of the message I was about to receive.

"It must be Jennie," I said throwing aside the blankets, rising to duty, so quick to return to that role, the way any mother in the middle of a sound sleep can do. "Her croup must be worse."

"Oh," Laurel said. Flat. Flat. Standing in the bright winter light reflected in the bedroom, unable to speak the words, herself, that would take my father from me.

As I scuffed down the cold stairs, I said, "I wonder if I need to go home." My cousin did not speak, though she followed me closely as I went to the phone. She stood, her shoulder almost touching mine, as she watched me listen to my husband's gentle voice, "Kate, I'm so sorry. Your father has died."

My knees buckled. I believe that is the phrase people use. They simply let go. Forgot what it is that knees do. I leaned over against her desk to hold myself up, one hand pressing the

phone to my ear as if I could not hear, and the other covering
my head in protection against the blow.

"It's okay," I said nodding my head, rapidly, insanely. "I
knew this would happen, you know? I knew." It was as if all of
the work of my life, all the hours I spent hyper-attending to my
father's illnesses, burning back the fields that threatened to
overtake our land, dreading this death day I had been fearing
my whole life—staring it right in its lousy face—could make
me prepared for it.

But it didn't prepare me.

I ran from the phone to the bathroom where I threw up all
over the toilet, all over the floor. I moaned and wailed like
women in news clips from foreign lands, suddenly woozy, dizzy,
spinning into the universe of all loss.

Laurel led me to the couch, handed me a brown paper bag
and made me breathe in, breathe out. She's a good nurse, that
cousin of mine. Even when we were little kids, she was right
there with a cold cloth if anyone felt sick. And how many little
cotton swabs did she dip into the brown peroxide bottle to
clean the million scrapes of our bike riding and tree climbing?

She shifted again now into that able, familiar mode and
moved me competently through the first moments of my dead
father.

Then I had this thought that maybe Roy had gotten it
wrong. It was a mix-up. "I have to call Richie," I said throwing
aside the crumpled paper bag and getting to my feet. Richie
would know. He, the steadiest of us kids. I had to talk to him.

I dialed our parents' number and he answered on the first
ring. "Rich?" I said. I bit down hard on my lip to steady my
chin, which felt like it had come undone from the rest of my
face.

"It finally happened," he said. Then, there was a moment

where neither of us spoke. The weight of those words was too much.

"Where's Mom?" I asked.

"She's right here," he said. "Kate?" He breathed in. "They took Dad, Kate. The ambulance just left."

Already? They took him? He was dead: that was one thing. But Jesus, please. Stop this. Who took him? My Dad. I am never going to see him again. Could everyone just slow down?

My mother came to the phone. "Hi, Hon," she said, her voice so soft, so calmed and disconnected sounding, that I feared she would simply float away before I could reach her.

"Does Peter know?" I asked and she told me he had a flight into Boston at six A.M. Could we pick him up?

Then she began to cry. "Oh, Kate, it was so awful." She started to sob. "I never wake up at night and I woke up because I felt he wasn't beside me, and I heard the shower running, and I called out to him, 'Dick, are you all right?' " Her voice heaved as she struggled for words and breath. "And all of a sudden I realized that I had been hearing that shower for a long time. That in my sleep, I had heard it running and running. And I knew, Kate. I knew before I even went in there."

I stretched my hand across the desk where I stood, reaching for her, because I needed to hold my mother, but my mother was miles away.

Because I couldn't myself, Laurel drove me back to my house, to Roy and the girls. And as we drove through that night; the moon was bright, and sharp, and unrelenting in its aliveness when my father was dead. Gone already, before I could even get home.

It was impossible to be still. At times I had my head out the window as if the problem with my irregular breathing was that there was not air enough in the car. As if I needed the freezing February wind in my face to get my lungs to work.

And then suddenly nausea overtook me again and I heaved dryly, unable to stop my body from its spasms.

"Would it help if you put your head on my lap?" Laurel asked me quietly.

And like I did when I was a little girl, I lay my head down, and was quieted by gentleness. And I knew, even then, that it was a mercy in my life that I was with Laurel, the woman I had loved since we were babies together in a crib.

That it was a mercy to be taken care of by her. My young children had not had to hear the wails of their mother's sorrow; my husband, who had always feared what this particular moment might do to me, was spared those initial hours.

"Look up at that moon, Kate," Laurel whispered. And I sat up and stared at it, knowing that neither of us would ever forget the way it lit the sky that particular night.

And Emmylou Harris was singing from the tape player, *"Praise God, I feel like singing, I'm on the other side of life now."* But there was no praise in my body. There was only terror at the suddenness that hurled him to the other side, which suddenly doesn't seem so sweet and reassuring. Because it is where you are not. It is where you cannot be.

The sharpness of death that steals your Dad when you aren't paying attention.

And I watched that moon as if it might be able to help. I wanted to reach my arm, high in the air, and pull it to me.

I thought of my father, the summer of the crows, standing out by the tallest pine. I thought of him reaching and calling, "Hello, crow. Hello, crow." And the way they would fly down to him from places I couldn't see.

I wondered if I called to him now, might he come back to us, like a bird across that bright, crescent moon? Might he come back? And be with us. Still.

# CHAPTER TWELVE

# The
# Hi-There
# Café

MY MOTHER AND I WAITRESSED together at the Hi-There. We wore white polyester uniforms that stained easily, and good sneakers so we wouldn't slip as we rushed around. My mother is the best waitress I've ever known. Friendly, with a little sass mixed in. Quick with a joke. Quick with the pot for a refill of coffee. (She'd be at your table two gulps before you'd motion to her to bring some more.) She was the most attentive to the timing of an order. None of this one meal served now, then five minutes later, the rest of them. And she was always willing to clean off my table stacked with greasy dishes, and wipe it down all nice, if she saw I was too busy to get right to it. "Kate, I'm going to take that deuce in the corner for you. Just get them their waters and I'll do the rest."

Let me tell you, you don't get that with every waitress you meet.

My mother made me look better at waitressing than I really

was. Though I was pretty darn good. It's just that no one was as good as her. I liked the job though, keeping my slips in order. Carrying four big plates of food stacked up my arm, hand to elbow, and a big, sweating pitcher of ice water in my free hand. I liked when people noticed my balancing abilities. I worked at how high I could get the swirl of whipped cream on a slice of pie.

I liked waiting on the locals. Tom and Loretta walked up for the fish fry every weekend and left a good tip. I even liked the tourists. Most of them. The ones who came to the Hi-There were not snobby, like the ones who went to the expensive restaurants in town. Our customers, even the ones from Massachusetts, appreciated a good meatloaf and mashed potato, a dish of tapioca pudding. Ten cups of coffee to wash it all down.

My favorite customers, though, were the truckers. They sat at the chrome-edged counter and stared ahead at the shelves of shiny water glasses turned upside down on a paper placemat with a map of New Hampshire on it. They played with the packets of sugar and the toothpicks. If it wasn't too busy I would ask about their road trips. What interested me was this: these guys would eat a BLT with a side of fries and a coffee shake, extra thick please, served by me one night in Moultonboro, New Hampshire. And then the next night, they'd be all the way out west in Cleveland, Ohio.

Okay, maybe Cleveland, Ohio isn't *out west*. But to folks in Moultonboro it was.

My parents' good friends, Art and Nat Lively, owned The Hi-There. Every morning, at exactly 7:00, my father drove the half-mile up to the Hi-There and had breakfast with Art.

He sat in the help's booth, the one in the corner by the

swinging kitchen door. Really, he considered it *his* booth. After all, his mug (nobody else better dare touch it) hung there next to Art's on special hooks they rigged just for this purpose.

My Dad and Art sang together in The Society for the Preservation and Encouragement of Barbershop Quartet Singing in America. Their mugs had a red-and-white barbershop pole printed on them and the yellow initials, SPEBQSA. Not the most accessible of acronyms. But they were proud of their society.

If I was working the breakfast shift, I'd bring my Dad his toast, his two poached eggs, and bacon (which he would send back unless it was practically burned). When it wasn't real busy, I'd sit down with him for a while. Jump up to get him his coffee when he was ready for more.

It was Art and Nat's place. But my Dad thought of it as his place too.

When my mother and I were on the night shift together, Dad and Richie would come in for supper. If there was a long line of customers all the way out the door, my father and brother would just say excuse me and head right on in to their booth in the corner. My mother would take their order. They didn't need menus. She'd race around, waiting on six tables at a time (and the whole counter if I didn't get to it quickly enough), and stop by my Dad's booth for a quick drag of his smoke as she hurried by with an armload of plates.

Because my Dad was president of the Barbershoppers at that time, and Art was vice president, a lot of their singing friends stopped in to the restaurant. Sometimes they did a little pickup. That's when barbershop guys get together whatever voices are available and just start singing. A single note would sound from the pitch pipe someone always seemed to be carrying in his pocket, and then they would break out into this tight, strong harmony on old songs so tender they could make you cry. Songs like "That Old Gang of Mine" and "Way Down Upon the Swanee River," and my Dad's favorite, "Alexander's Ragtime Band."

On the days when barbershoppers weren't around, my mother and I fed our tip quarters into the jukebox and listened to Perry Como and the Andrews Sisters. My mother sang as she worked. No one minded at all.

When I think of it now, I think about how often my family sang. How often we were together in the living room by the hot wood stove while it snowed outside. Or the nights we spent in the old, hand-hewn shed off the kitchen that we fixed up as our summer living room. It was crowded with Dad's collection of old barbershop relics, and the wooden pegged farm tools he searched out. An assortment of lumpy old couches and ladder-back chairs. We would sit there late into the night, singing and laughing at the occasional bat swooping down at us.

We sang Ernest Tubb and Patsy Cline. We sang Jim Reeves and George Jones. We have all loved Emmylou Harris ever since Peter brought home one of her first records back in the early seventies. At first we thought she might be weird, not real country. But once we heard "We've All Got Wheels to Take Ourselves Away," we were set.

At the end of the night when the last customers in the Hi-There finally cleared out, my mother and I would turn up the jukebox and sing as loud as we wanted. Then we would wipe down the counters one last time. Fill the salt and pepper shakers. Sweep good under all the red vinyl booths, around the chairs and tables cleaning up dropped butter pat papers, tangled straw wrappers, and empty sugar packets wadded up like spitballs.

We would sit ourselves down at the corner booth. She would have a smoke and I would have a tall glass of water. We'd count up the wads of dollar bills and jangle of quarters stuffed in the pockets of our aprons, making neat piles on the table before us. Art and Nat would come by to lock up the doors. Then we'd head home.

Some nights it would be so hot and mosquito-ey we couldn't sleep. I'd hear her downstairs and I would join her in the kitchen where she sat in one of my Dad's T-shirts with her sore legs up on a kitchen chair. I'd put my feet up too. We would talk about the customers we'd had that night. Or sometimes we'd make a salad and eat it just to cool off.

Finally, we would unwind: the noise of piling plates, the kitchen shouts of "Order! Pick up!" and the sound of banging doors would start to fade.

My mother would head to her room and crawl in next to my snoring Dad. I would head out to the back porch to the bunk beds we had set up for nights as hot as those. The sounds of crickets and bullfrogs soon replaced the sounds of the diner. The stars scattered across the sky blurred before my tired eyes. I let go, once more, of a good night's work, and slept.

# CHAPTER THIRTEEN

# Then, Without My Father

THE SNOW WAS FALLING, slow motion. A sudden wind shifted the curtain of snow and I could see Red Hill. He was gone, but our hill was still there. I wondered what else remained unchanged.

Then it was three days already after the service, and none of us could seem to remember how to sleep. We were loopy with grief and fatigue. There were too many people stopping by. All that food to find room for in the already crowded refrigerator.

The visitors whispered, conspiratorially, that the best thing to help my mother was to get my father's clothes right out of the house. The job would only get harder. So my brothers and I went up to Ellen's General Store for cardboard boxes.

Roy and Peter and I stood in the middle of the room among the empty boxes, looking around. Do we take the framed photographs and the little brass tray with his tie clip and change, and the small leather box full of his treasures from his bureau? The ones that have been there, just like that, our whole lives? But Richie started right in. He went into the bathroom and started pulling everything out of the cabinet over my father's sink. The shaving things, the little scissors he used to trim his mustache, all the bottles of pills we had hoped would stave off the bursting pain in his poor head. The nicotine patches he had used for only fifteen days. Did it kill him to have to quit smoking? Or was it just a move he made too late?

My mother went to his top drawer, took two of his T-shirts and walked, quietly, to her own bureau. She tucked them there among her nightgowns. None of us said a word.

The night he died, Dad had taken off his jeans and folded them neatly over the chair at his desk near the window of the bedroom. He had removed his flannel shirt and hung it, too, over the chair. The arms hung down so if you walked in the room, quickly, not really thinking clearly, it could look for a moment like he was sitting there.

It would take years before I would stop seeing him in that house.

I stood at his desk, trying to force myself to clear it off. Everyone else was working hard. I needed to help too. I regarded his organization: the separation of paper clips by size, the sharpened pencils all pointing the same way, the neat stacks of papers with his precise handwriting.

I reached down to his chair. A lovely, old wooden chair he had recently polished, and I slipped his shirt from the place where, really, he had only just placed it—expecting another day of wear. I held the shirt to my nose. His particular scent had not yet been taken. I breathed it in. Oh, Dad.

By the time we finished our cleaning, we were nauseated with exhaustion. The room looked peculiar and bare. My mother lay down on her bed and we, her children, stood around her aware of the awful, empty space beside her. We watched as she regarded the bathroom where just a few nights ago she had found her husband dead on the floor. That bathroom door was the first thing she saw from where she lay on the bed.

"Let's change the room around," Richie said suddenly. Without waiting for our response, he started pulling out chairs and bureaus.

We took apart the bed and moved it over near the window where the sun would shine in each morning and where our mother could watch it set over Red Hill each afternoon. Where she had at least a chance of not imagining, again, her husband dead on the floor the first thing when she opened her eyes.

When we finished, Richie had to leave for work. My mother needed to try to sleep. But Peter and I were hyper with something we couldn't name. He said, "Let's go to Laconia and get some new things for this bedroom." We talked her into going with us and helped her out to the car.

It is a curious thing to go back out in the world after death. People were going on with their lives, pumping gas, pulling up to the drive-in window at the bank, putting groceries in their trunks. As if Dick Young wasn't dead at all. They bought movie tickets, and sat waiting for haircuts in the grimy chairs of Bill's Barbershop as if it were just another day.

At Kmart, we grabbed a carriage and headed to Domestics. There was a whole aisle of all this new Martha Stewart stuff. My mother loved Martha Stewart. We were jubilant: we had found something that helped. We picked out the kind of flowered sheets my mother loves but my father would never have wanted. We got pillowcases and pillow shams and five different tossed pillow accessories. There were bathroom things to match, for the goodness sakes, so we got the little soap dish, the little cup, and hand towels too.

Then we looked up at my mother and saw that she was about to pass out.

"I have to get out of here," she said.

Peter took her arm and helped her outside while I went to the checkout counter with our overflowing cart.

The cashier smiled, not insincerely, and said, "How are you today?"

I took her at her word. That she was really asking about me, not just saying what you say when a person comes to your register.

I said, "My father died this week. I . . . I don't know what to do."

I looked at the cashier, saw the trace of alarm in her eyes, and stopped myself from saying anything more.

I watched her exaggerated concentration as she rang up the sheets, pillows, towels. The pretty little matching cup and dish. "That will be $257.89," she said and I handed over my credit card.

The cashier and I fumbled with the huge plastic bags of new matching Martha Stewart home décor items and I realized, miserably, sickeningly, that this probably wouldn't help after all.

Another week passed, and grief still choked my voice so I could not always speak, choked my throat so I could not eat, and it wound around my mind so I could not remember what I had been doing—*what did I come into this room for?*

I needed to start paying more attention to my children. I walked with my oldest daughter on the dirt road from my parents' house. Or did I now have to call it my mother's house? Was he erased in that way as well?

There was a suggestion of coming warmth in the air, a trace of mud among the ice in the road. When we got to the landing the snow was so shiny and white it was like seven-minute boiled frosting, poured over the world. We walked home across the frozen pond and it felt like the magic it was—walking on water.

There is still beauty, I thought. And I was so grateful that not everything had been taken.

My daughter drew me three pictures in the snow with a stick as tall as she was. A picture of a cup of coffee with steam coming from it. A big heart with the words *I Love You* written inside. And a blackboard and desk because I love to teach.

This was her best effort to bring her mother back. For a few moments it helped.

Then it was time to return home to the city and resume life there. The Lenten season had just begun. Roy and I took the girls to church, easing ourselves back into important routines. It was all so bleak with the starkness of the season. Stark hymns, stark words.

My husband asked me what I was giving up for Lent. I was shocked at the suggestion that I should participate this year. "I am giving up my father," I said. He regarded my ire, and nodded. "That is probably really true."

Our oldest girl, Elizabeth, was back at kindergarten. I worried about standing there with the mothers waiting for the school doors to open. Sympathy from others would weaken me. Kindness hurt. But then I worried, too, that there wouldn't be enough understanding. I needed for people to know that this was not just another death. Not simply another sad thing in a world of sad things.

This was a death I feared my whole life.

The newspaper said he died suddenly. But it wasn't sudden at all. It began when I was just a small child. Now that he was finally, truly dead, could I believe his death would ever stop?

It wouldn't stop. He continued to die when I heard a song

he liked, or when my youngest girl, Jennie, did something he would have laughed about, or when spring came again. A spring he would not see.

I talked to my doctor about getting some medication to make my heart stop racing. "Of course," she said. "This is very natural."

I went back to teach my class for elder students on writing their life stories. Verne Rachel, one of my favorite older women, came up to me in the hall where I stood outside the classroom not daring to go in. She would die soon of leukemia and knew it.

"Be courageous," she said and took hold of my shoulders to force me to look her in the eye. When I lifted my face to hers, she nodded. Then hugged her old body to mine.

What helped the most was to walk. To walk hard. Uphill. My cousins came to make me do it. Laurel, Cheryl, Katherine, and Mary. The walking loosened the flutter that burned in my chest. In my heart.

Walking helped. And also baths. Hot, soaking baths in a tub full of water and tears.

And it helped to lie beside my husband at night and feel the warmth of his body as he slept next to me. As I began to try to believe that he would not die too.

It was many months before my mother was able to spread my father's ashes. Then one morning in late May my mother woke before dawn, as had become the pattern of her widowhood. She called Leanie and said, "I'm going to do it."

"Well, you aren't going alone," Leanie said. "Come on over and get me."

"But it's not even light out."

"I've been waking up before light ever since Ding died," my mother's best friend said. "Come on over."

So they drove together, in the cold car, over to the one little store in Center Harbor that opened early for the road crew guys going off to work. They bought Styrofoam cups of coffee, covering them with plastic lids.

My mother set hers in the cup holder of her car, next to the box of her husband's ashes. She took a deep breath and the two friends looked at each other. Then drove toward the farm where we used to live.

My mother pulled down the dirt driveway and parked the car outside the house other people now owned. But it had been our home. And she knew how much my father had loved it.

She picked up the box, opened the plastic bag, and carefully took a handful of the ashes. Leanie did the same. Their hands were trembling. It was dark still. The owners inside were no doubt asleep, unaware of the widows in their yard.

They knelt next to my father's lilacs, the ones he had dug up from the farm where he spent his boyhood summers in Maine. Lilacs he and Peter had planted at the end of the brick walk they laid themselves. Spring comes slowly to New Hampshire, the lilacs were not yet fully in bloom.

My mother's hand shook as she held it in the air above the cold ground. Then she opened her fist and let go. Some of the ashes stuck to her hand, sweating as she was, even in the cold of that spring dawn. But some fell upon the lilac roots he had dug, and watered, and loved.

Then they walked over to the stonewall of the pasture and spread some ashes there. On the wide boards of the barn floor. Out near where the chicken coop had once stood. Then they walked slowly away.

My mother kept the headlights off as she backed her car out onto the road. She drove to the house she and my father had built for their retirement. She and Leanie went to the kitchen table and sat where they had sat through every happy and tragic event of their shared lives.

My mother pulled the plastic lid from her coffee. It was still hot. Had it taken so short a time to do this thing she had to do, that it had not even cooled?

The two friends cried all morning. Cried for the husbands they had lost. Cried for the way they would have to outlive them now.

Slowly, my mother finished her coffee. It was the only thing that seemed to taste good to her anymore. And then she cried again. For about the thousandth time that spring.

In those early days I was so afraid that my husband would die also. I waited at the door for him at night, needing to learn that you really can say goodbye to a person in the morning and have them come back again at night.

I was playing through in my mind what I would do if anything happened to Roy. How would I ever survive without this man, my husband and friend, and the way only he knows me? What would I do? Whom could I call?

My brother, Richie. I would call him. I pictured him sitting at his desk, where he was now the chief of police in our hometown. I imagined his desk, as neat as Dad's, and realized that he was the person I could always call for help.

I got thinking about how he was the one who was right there to help Mom the night Dad died. How he had moved the huge oak table where we had eaten all those holiday and birthday dinners, all those everyday suppers. How he had just pulled it out of the way, like it was balsa, so the coroners could get in with their stretcher.

How he had gone in and helped my mother clean up our Dad. He protected people's dignity. And how he stayed in our hometown for those reasons.

I dialed the number at the station and Ginny put me right through to him.

"Hey, Rich," I said and he could probably hear that I was crying.

"Everything okay?" he asked, ever on duty.

"Yah," I said and swallowed a sob. "I was sitting here, though, thinking I wouldn't know how to live if anything ever happened to Roy—what would I do, you know? And I realized I could call you. You'd come right down. Be here in three hours," I swallowed another sob. "It just really means a lot to me that I can count on you like that."

"Well," he said. I wondered if I had gotten too emotional on him, as I sometimes do with my brother.

"I know you have to get back to work," I said nervously. "I'll let you go."

"Hey, Kate," he said just as I was about to hang up. "Just so we understand each other, I can make that trip in just over two hours."

"Okay," I said, somewhere between chuckling and crying.

"Okay," he said. "That's it then."


And this is how we have found our way without my father. One move and then another. Some of them worked. Some of them didn't. But each attempt has carried us further along in this life without him. Most times, we are able to figure out a way to help each other. At least a little.

Then there are times when we trip on loss because he's gone. So gone. There is no denying it. My father is dead. I know that.

But for me, he will never stop dying.

# CHAPTER FOURTEEN

# I Love to Tell the Story

I LOVED SUNDAY SCHOOL. I loved the little rooms with child-sized tables and chairs painted bright colors. I loved the teachers who told us stories, the crafts, and the shiny stick-on star we received for every week we came. Each classroom had a poster board with a carefully drawn line for each of the children's names, followed by a whole row of boxes for every Sunday of the year.

For the child whose parents bring her each week this is a triumph. Star after star, row after row. But for the child for whom empty little boxes are more prevalent than the occasional, measly bit of shine, these poster boards are a grim reminder of what isn't working.

And now, I am a Sunday school teacher myself, leading the children toward God. I smile a lot, and give a lot of hugs, and welcome the ones who come every week. Especially, I welcome the children who don't. I understand trouble with attendance.

And it satisfies an old need in me to be especially generous to the ones who can't seem to get there. You won't see attendance boards in any of our classrooms. To me, they don't seem to be the point.

And to the people of my church, I look like I know exactly what I'm doing. Like I've never been far from the classroom: growing in God, year after glorious year. That lovely Mrs. Caley. Who else would she have grown up to be but the head of our wonderful children's worship center? But no, that is not my story.

I am here now to give the children who come my way some things that I didn't get when I was their age. I extend to them a bit of love as unconditional as I can muster. I show them that they are as welcome as anyone at God's house. And I try to show this even if they only come once because I realize this may be all they are getting of God for a while.

That's how it was for me. Even after we stopped regularly going to church, my parents would sometimes find a service to take us to for Christmas Eve or Easter. And I think of those times now, when I hear people speak disparagingly about "Christmas and Easter Christians" who march right into churches like they own the place, taking up the pews of the more faithful attendees.

But I know this. It is not that those people think they own the place. It is that they are trying so hard to fit in—and they are so glad to be back—that they march in so they will look like they know what they are doing. They want so much to be-long—they know everyone can see they don't.

And when you are a kid, you can only get there when some-one helps to get you there.

One fall Mrs. Owens stopped by to take me with her up to the Methodists. I loved their portable classroom dividers and

Mrs. Owens' gentle ways, but I wasn't so familiar with their hymns and nobody really seemed to know me the way I was used to being known, so I stopped going.

The next year, Cindi Tolman, one of our best neighbors, had a Good News Club at her house on Goss Corner. We were allowed to get off the school bus at her house every Thursday and sit in her clean living room and sing fun songs. She had sent away by mail for the shiny, Good News handouts that I carried home proudly and hung on my bedroom wall.

One year, my Aunt Elinor took me to the Vacation Bible School at her church in Massachusetts, the one that my mother had grown up in. There I learned the song, "Peace, Be Still," a song I still sing sometimes when I am afraid. I also learned the important Vacation Bible School art of constructing the Popsicle stick jewelry box, and decorating an empty bleach bottle with brightly colored rickrack to transform it into a toilet brush holder. What these particular crafts had to do with our Lord, I cannot exactly tell you. But I know this: there were women there who helped me, gladly, with the awkward swipes of glue; and who served homemade cookies and as many cups of thinned-out juice as I could drink.

They were women who remembered singing with my mother in the choir before she moved to New Hampshire and they asked me—did she still sing alto? I couldn't bring myself to say, "Well, she would, but they kicked her out." I just smiled at the thought of her in a light blue choir robe that matched everyone else's.

After the Vacation Bible School that year, I came back home to New Hampshire with my sights set higher, ready to keep on with the important truths I'd learned from our colorful memory verse handouts.

But where do you go with your Popsicle stick jewelry box

and memory verses? And how do you keep on if no one offers the ride to where you need to go to learn more?

Was there no one who noticed that I really, really missed church? That I was sad? Ate a lot? Slept a lot? Or did I look like a kid who was okay, the way a kid who really is not okay can do? I rode the snowmobile my father and Ding Martin bought us, in and out of the lines of apple trees; learned to dive in a cold lake; opened nice birthday presents as the years went past; won first, and sometimes second or third prize, for the chickens and quail we entered in the Fair up in Sandwich each year. Maybe I looked like everything was fine. But how I wished someone had recognized my need to be in church.

And now, I'm the teacher trying every week to find a way to reach the kids whose home lives make it hard for them to get to church.

I think particularly of three tough kids who started coming all by themselves. They had to take two city bus routes to get to us. Had never been in a church before. And it showed.

There were three of them, two sisters and their brother. Shauna, enormous for fourteen, always in a winter coat as big as a man's. Jamal was her angry twelve-year-old brother whom nobody could get along with. And then there was Laura. Laura was eleven. She looked like a tenth grader and read like a first grader, a source of crushing embarrassment. Laura is the one I can't seem to forget.

When they showed up week after week, honestly, I was not glad to see them. I had too much to do, keeping the bored kids I already had from becoming more bored. I hardly needed the addition of these kids who couldn't even spell *Jesus*. I was busy. Efficient. My over-functioning Sunday school director self. I simply didn't have time.

They kept coming though. Maddeningly good attendance,

those kids. So all that fall they learned the stories of Jesus—all the best ones: the wine at the wedding, the loaves and fishes, the healing of the blind man with spit and dirt.

And then, we learned about the one that became Laura's favorite. The day she started loving Jesus was when I told them about the woman caught in adultery.

By this time, I was slowly starting to catch on about how to get through to the children. I had abandoned the stick-the-apostle's-head-on-the-dotted-line handouts. We began to act out the stories. That day, one girl volunteered to sit on the floor as the woman caught in adultery. I asked the other children to ball up their papers and make them into rocks to throw at this bad woman, the one who broke The Law. But Laura didn't want to do it.

And then there was Jamal. I asked him to be Jesus, writing words in the sand and then lifting his head with the gentle, good reply, *"Let he who is without sin, throw the first stone."*

Laura loved it. She got it. That story about Jesus' goodness became her own.

A few weeks later, I was rattling off our Lenten agenda in my busy, efficient way. I tapped my pencil, put my hand firmly on the shoulder of a boy who wouldn't behave, and said, "We'll do three more miracles, Palm Sunday, The Triumphal Entry to Jerusalem, and then it's The Crucifixion." A deep breath of accomplishment on my part. I was really moving them through the church year.

Laura looked up from a fingernail she was biting. "The *cru-* what?"

I didn't comprehend her question, but one of the other children responded, "The crucifixion. When they killed Him." That child had been in my class for three years straight and had this stuff down pat.

We all looked at Laura to see if she was done with all her questions and interrupting.

How can I help you hear the desperation in Laura's voice as she spoke? "They . . . killed . . . Him?"

Can I explain the look on her face as I stared across the table where she sat beyond my reach? I had to slow down, way down, to meet that child in her horror. *Stop the lesson, Kate. Stop the cramming, the view of the whole thing as regular and rote, as something we all know already anyway.*

I looked across that Sunday school table at Laura, reached for her. "You're going to love the way this story ends," I said to her and told her what I know.

In that moment I learned that what goes on in a Sunday school is not about me, nor any intentions I might have. It is not about whether children know their Bible or attend regularly or not.

It is all about a relationship that is between each one of us and Him who created us and calls us by name. Our true Teacher, the One with the gentle, good reply. He is the redeemer who takes what is broken in all of our lives and hands it back to us, transformed.

It's this amazing, lifelong process—that has its mistakes, like my unthinking rushing with Laura at such an important moment—and that has times of being so right, so close to Him, that all else seems to fall away into that Light.

I would like to be able to tell you that Laura and her brother and sister are growing beautifully now in our children's worship center. The truth is they stopped coming.

Maybe I tried a couple of times to get in touch with them. Or maybe I got too busy. I don't want to remember. But here's the deal. The relationship those children began with God goes beyond the confines of place, and certainly beyond any effectiveness or ineffectiveness on my part.

For a long time, I felt so guilty about failing them. I still look for Laura, sometimes, as I drive around the city. And wait for her to come back to All Saints so I can do it right.

But just as the search for God began and stopped in me many times, I am counting on more to come for Laura. Maybe that's simplistic. But I know what I've seen. What she received the day we acted out the story of the forgiven woman nobody gets to take away.

# CHAPTER FIFTEEN

# Pictures We Don't Take

I WAS VISITING MY BEST FRIEND, Carole, out in Michigan. I had brought a stack of photographs to update her on my life since I had seen her last. Over a morning cup of coffee I showed her the scenes from my life. There were pictures of my girls' birthday parties and of Christmas. There were a couple of the new paint job in the living room and a handful from a hike we had taken in New Hampshire. There was one my father had taken the summer before he died of my two brothers and me standing together at the Fourth of July parade in our hometown.

Later that evening, after we had our daughters settled in for the night, we shared a bottle of wine on her porch. "On the porch" is our shorthand for the state of mind we are in and the conversations that we have there. Conversations that happen only when we are with each other, when it is late at night, and we are loosened by wine and fatigue, and the lack of interruptions by kids and phones, and the details of the daytime.

After lighting candles to scent the air and snuggling down in our chairs, I began to tell her about some trouble that was brewing in my marriage. Trouble that was typical, predictable even. But it didn't feel that way to me. It just felt hard. I started to cry.

"Pictures we don't take," she said as she poured herself another glass of wine. I didn't understand so she continued. "All morning you showed me the pictures from your life, as if *they* were your life. But not one of them showed what you are telling me: the pictures we don't take."

I am thinking these days about the idea of pictures we don't take. I think about the pictures I have only in the form of memories. The ones I shape into images with my words.

My father, for example. Do I show all the ways there are to look at him? Or do I show only the charming dreamer? A man who knew that there were more important things than the security that would have been his if he had stayed with his grandfather's company outside of Boston?

Do I show the photograph of what those dreams cost my mother? That she had to waitress, often seven nights a week for weeks at a stretch, lifting heavy trays and waiting on impatient tourists for their lousy tips?

I want the image of the wet, slippery edge of the pond down behind our house—and how we would take our city cousins down the hill in the summer to throw handfuls of dusty cracked corn to the mallards and wood ducks that were my Dad's favorites. And I want a photograph of the rigged up long extension cords with a big light and all of us cousins skating on that pond, late into the night, during our February school vacations.

Or the scene where I was eight years old, alone at night in a vast barn, with only one dim bulb hanging on a wire to illumine my way with the heavy pail of water I carried to our cow. I want to frame the photograph of that small, brave girl.

Or this one. Sometimes my mother would have a little extra grocery money for the week. She would bring home baloney, and cellophane packages of our favorite cookies, and boxes of macaroni, five for a dollar. And every now and then, she bought a pomegranate for special.

We would sit at the kitchen table after we helped her put away the groceries, enjoying the look of those full cupboards. And she would split open the pomegranate, with her just painted nails, and give us all a hunk, even Richie when he was a baby. And we worked our tongues into the little holes and sucked out the juice and what sweet there was, and we would laugh, all of us, at the tiny bits of fruit and the fruit stains on Richie's white baby T-shirt, and my mother would laugh too. And light a cigarette and be happy. I want that picture.

And the one of that incredible morning, the day my father brought home ninety-nine chickens. We carried all those different birds into our coop, watching them strut across the concrete floor, investigating the fresh floor shavings for bits of feed we scattered.

But then I must also remember the lonely shot of my mother as she stood in the dirt driveway watching my father and brothers and me unload crate after crate of hens. There were bantams, and Rhode Island Reds, and Buff Cochins, and even a couple of Aroucanas.

I would have to remember her by the lilacs, standing in the long calico skirt and peasant blouse she wore to work, shaking her head at this dream of his.

"But they were *free*, June," my father said to my mother's silence. "And just think what a great learning experience this is for the kids."

"Dick," she said before she turned to walk back into the house. "We can't even afford groceries. Where are you going to find the money to feed those lousy chickens?"

I remember that dusk came slowly when I was a child, and that evening smelled like meadow grass and sweat and granite from the stone walls we walked across barefoot, scraping our soft toes on the crusty lichen.

But there are other memories too.

Here is an image seared in my brain I would like to tear into a million pieces. This one. My father kept a spare pack of Parliaments hidden behind a decorative copper mold on the kitchen wall. It was his emergency pack in case the cartons he bought every other day should fail him. He would check behind that copper mold, every now and then, just to be sure the pack was there.

My Dad was a smoker. I don't just mean he smoked. I mean he *cut back* to four packs a day when the doctor yelled at him and refused to ever see him again.

And it is true that one of the strongest memories I have of my father is of our walks around the farm, me holding his big, warm hand, as we checked on pens of pheasants or sheep.

But another of my strongest memories is this: he had to get up a few times—in the middle of the night—to smoke. And if you asked my brothers or me we could easily describe that familiar scene: the little red circle of the glow, just illuminating his large hand, as he sat on the edge of the bed. Every night he was there, bent over with his elbows on his knees, eyes closed, sucking that cigarette at three o'clock in the morning.

"Hi, Dad," I'd whisper on my way to the bathroom to pee. And he would turn and lift the little red glow in greeting, and maybe smile.

Every scene I've ever written about him, and will write about him, is true—he really did raise chicks that scurried across the kitchen table and floors; and wake us in the middle of the night to see a wet calf get pulled from its heaving mother. But there are other true things.

Another picture is the one that shows what this writing has cost my mother. It appears we are this strong mother and daughter pair, talking through our past, doing the hard work—together—becoming even closer in the process.

And that is true. But I have caused pain in my mother's life by my questions.

She told me so. She said not everyone is able to look back at their life and uncover all the pieces. She told me to be careful about expecting that of everyone—it just doesn't go that way.

We were having our morning coffee together and she said, "The difference between me and some people is not the amount of pain in our lives. Many people have many kinds of pain. But I have faced mine. I have faced the hardest things, Kate. And I keep going."

She looked at me with strength and satisfaction. Her beautiful eyes were shining.

When I think about the photograph I want to show my daughters, it is my mother's face in that moment. The image of the hardest things that happened blending with joy. Joy she chooses. And teaches me to choose as well.

# CHAPTER SIXTEEN

# The Groaning Ice of the New Year

I WAS BACK IN MY hometown recently, back with the pine-woods that surround my mother's house, the frozen pond. Christmas was over and New Year's just days away. Roy and the girls and I packed up our snow gear and favorite presents (the ones Elizabeth and Jennie couldn't possibly live without for five days) and headed north. We all needed the lack of noise, and traffic lights, and phone calls from people with things they wanted us to do.

I wanted to give in to that childhood sense of endless hours: reading, walking in the woods, napping. Watching, each day at exactly 4:03—as if by magic—the deep, inexplicable shades of blue purple and orange pink melt into a winter sunset.

As I quieted myself I pondered the question that I couldn't seem to shake: who was it who kicked us out of the church? My mother had told me everything she was able to about the vote against her. "Hon," she finally said to me after another long and tearful conversation, "it was such a bad, bad time—it's just too hard for me to remember anymore. I can't do it."

But couldn't someone remember? If I could see the actual scene in my mind, maybe the cold grip of its power would ease. I couldn't stand the thought of every hand in the room going up in vote against her. Or the scene I imagined when she walked out the double doors from the church where once everyone had loved us. Was she trembling?

And was my father a comfort? Did he take her for a drive up the Ben Berry Road and down around Ossipee Mountain, his response to so many kinds of trouble? Did he tell her he would stand by her no matter what? Even though it meant he couldn't be a minister anymore; that position he had worked so hard to achieve?

It is the thought of my mother alone, unwanted, that un- does me.

Recently, though, I had learned that Cindi and Bill Tolman were with my parents that night. After so many years of not speaking that one profound detail, my mother loosened the memory and handed it over to me. She did not know that for me the scene then became bearable.

When my parents left the church, these friends were with them.

Now, when I imagine that night, I can see them all going back to the farm, making coffee, firing up the wood stove, maybe warming a frozen coffee cake, and talking around the kitchen table late in the night. I can imagine Cindi and my mother crying, and I can picture the hard-set jaws of Bill's and my father's anger.

But they were together. That is the difference.

I could now look back to those first hard months after the vote, remember Cindi and Bill's friendship to our family, and grasp its significance. Not everyone from the church had shunned us. It was like clearing jammed logs, and leaves, and ice from the frozen pump house by the brook and hearing the water rush suddenly in.

They had moved to the farm when we bought it in 1968—added their dream to our own—cast their lots with us, two by two. Cindi was eighteen years old and my favorite babysitter from church. She had just married Bill, an air force guy from Maine with a talent for baseball and carpentry. She wore her long hair tucked plainly behind her ears. It was years before she switched from skirts to pants like other young women her age. Bill kept his hair shorn in the air force style and wore sturdy, dark blue work pants with matching shirts. Everything about them seemed sensible. Functional.

How do I explain that the orderliness of their lives provided a shelter for me when so much in my life was out of order?

They rented the small cottage behind our barn (built originally for a farmhand) and set up their new life together. Cindi spruced up the run-down place, sewing curtains and planting flowers. Bill set up a workshop and rototilled a garden. They planted tomatoes, two kinds of beans and squash, and that fall Cindi filled colorful rows of canning jars for her winter cupboard.

It is these early tasks of their marriage that come to mind when I think of them now. They were hardworking, conservative, like a farm couple left over from the forties. They did life the way their grandparents had. Loved God. Got married. Worked hard.

Bill cleaned out a cobwebbed shed behind the barn and rigged a workbench along one side of the old wall. He attached jar lids to the bottom of narrow shelves he built, then twisted a small, clear jar onto each one. They hung in a line, nails sorted by size, shiny and ready. He owned every type of screwdriver made, every length and bit, and shiny saws that never dulled or rusted from being left out of doors overnight.

In our Dad's workshop, my brothers and I would go looking for a tool among the disarray we kids always left, and would be unable to find a saw (one had been forgotten in the dusty hayloft; another was left weeks earlier in the orchard while trying to perfect our tree house). But Bill didn't lose things like we did.

Neither did Cindi. Her tiny kitchen had a brand-new apartment stove and refrigerator that seemed child-sized, and magic, the stuff of storybooks. I wondered when I'd be old enough to move into that cottage myself. I'd fill glass parfaits with shiny, red and orange Jell-O and line them on the clean shelves of the new fridge, just like Cindi.

If I stopped by to visit, she would serve me a tall glass of real iced tea from her new Tupperware pitcher. She fixed it the slow way her grandmother in Arkansas had taught her, and served me the grown-up beverage like it was the most natural thing in the world.

She would show me whatever latest project she was making—cut out paper pumpkins to decorate her bulletin board or a new cotton apron—and sometimes she let me make things too. It was like having your favorite teacher live right with you.

After supper, Bill and my father would meet out by the stone wall; Dad having a cigarette, Bill leaning back against the stones, one barn boot crossed over the other, as he told stories about growing up in Maine. I remember the sound of their voices: the low, drawn-out syllables of New England, the quiet chuckle—that reserved way of two men enjoying each other's company, but not going all out to show it.

Sometimes I would go too and sit on the stone wall, the rough lichen scratching the back of my young legs. I would listen to their men talk. I could hear in the cadence of their words that men were sure of everything they said, their voices as deep as their opinions. I would sit on granite fit together a hundred years before—still holding strong—and it seemed from listening to my father and Bill that opinions were as sure and immovable as an old, stone wall.

But my mother and Cindi were not that way together. They weren't so absolutely sure about every single thing they did and thought. There was ease between them. That familiar ease of two women, sitting at a kitchen table with cups of tea, talking about their day. Talking about the things married women have always talked about. Babies and husbands and trouble along the way. They showed me the ways of women, not always sure of their opinions, but sure of the importance of sharing them.

I remember they were crazy and wonderful, sometimes. Lucy and Ethel at their best. I remember the sound when their whole bodies laughed.

There was the day I saw them running down the dirt road, my mother, still such a city girl, tripping on the hem of one of her pretty bathrobes, while Cindi tried to entice our two errant cows back to the barn by shaking a can of molasses feed. I remember my mother screaming when the cows turned and began to run toward her; and Cindi laughing, calling out, "They want the feed, not you!" as my mother jumped the stone wall to get away from the seeming stampede.

I remember Cindi walking down the whole length of the field with me so I could show her the roaring spring runoff at the brook's curve. She understood that it was worth the scratches on our legs, from the long grass and brambles, to see the water run. So much kindness, that woman. Patience. Qualities I would later label as gifts of the spirit. Back then I didn't have that language, but I knew I felt love when I was with her.

Within a couple of months of my parents leaving the church, Cindi and Bill decided to leave as well. As hard as it was for my family, it was harder yet for the young couple. While we had friends at the church, Cindi had connections that went even deeper. She had been a part of those people her whole life. To take herself from it was to take herself from the things she knew best.

But though she was only eighteen years old, she knew she could not stay. She had that in her. I wonder if I had been a woman in that town, in those pews, and made to vote—what would I have done?

And even more I wonder, what if no vote had been taken? No decisions against anyone. Just grace. God.

To how many generations do the actions of that one, particular winter extend?

Now, thirty years after the vote, I had asked Cindi and Bill to come over for supper with my mother and me. I had asked them to tell me what they remembered. They had not turned from us like everyone else. I wanted to know why.

I stood in my mother's kitchen and thickened the soup I had made the day before. I had torn the meat from the Christmas carcass, turning what remained into good soup for our friends. I chopped winter vegetables, noticing the gleam of peeled carrots, and the sting of onions in my eyes. I let the tears fall as if they were only about onions.

Really, I was crying with the possibility of understanding an old thing in a new way. The new year was coming. What would it bring?

I went into the living room where my mother sat on the sagging couch.

"I wonder how tonight will go," my mother said and I nodded casually. The visit just minutes away, we sat together quietly as if we weren't about to possibly hear something we might not want to know.

Six o'clock approached and I glanced at the door, suspecting they would be on time. My mother said to me, "Why don't we say a quick prayer before they get here?"

My mother had often said grace before family meals, especially since Dad died. And at my cousin Katherine's shower for those long-awaited babies, she had offered up the loveliest prayer of thankfulness I'd ever heard. But I do not know her to be a woman to pray out loud. For her. For me. She had sung to me—often—but this praying was a new thing.

"Our dear, heavenly Father," she began. This is how my mother always begins a prayer, "Our dear, heavenly Father." And her voice sounds so pretty when she prays. Softer. Maybe a little higher. It strikes me that having never known her father, who died when she was only two, it must be helpful to think of God this way. The father who never leaves.

She prayed for me and for my writing. She prayed that our friends would feel comfortable with the questions I would ask them. She prayed that it would not be too hard for Cindi. Then she said amen and smiled at me, my brave mother.

The doorbell rang and there they were. Our old friends. They were so familiar to me and yet I felt shy as we stood in the draft of the front door. Shy, because I live in the city now. I had not seen them since my father's funeral and I was about to invade the places where they put things.

We sat at the same kitchen table where they'd spent so many hours with my parents, playing cards and laughing. But now we were not completely sure what to do.

I carried bowls of hot turkey soup to the table. The simple ritual of eating brought familiar comfort.

After supper we went to sit in the living room. It was dark outside. No stars. No Red Hill to remind me where I was in relation to the world. I jumped in. I asked my questions. I asked if they remembered when my mother was kicked out.

I wanted this steady, practical couple to report that it wasn't as bad as my mother told me.

"Well, that would have been when we were in the honeymoon cottage," Bill said, speaking of our nickname for the tiny house behind our barn. "I don't remember the exact year but let's see, it had to be '68 or '69."

"It was right before I got pregnant with Jonathan," Cindi added. "I remember it was so cold, so it must have been winter."

My mother nodded, "February," she said, twisting her wide gold wedding band on her slender hand.

And so, thirty years later, we pieced together this shared history of ours. My father, that essential character, too long gone from us. Together Cindi and Bill worked out the dates, and remembered scenes I had forgotten, and I watched them, knowing as I always did as a child, that I could count on their help.

They told me that a business meeting had been called one evening. It wasn't during regular morning church. That they were sitting with my parents in the sanctuary of The First Church of God. "Brother Munroe would have been standing at the pulpit and would have called for someone to make a motion to withdraw fellowship from your mother. That's what the good old First Church of God called it. They didn't say they were kicking you out. They called it 'withdrawing fellowship.'"

Cindi said he'd have asked for someone to make a first and someone to second it. My mother said yes, that was right.

I felt my body react. Rapid breath. Rapid heart. I was close to something that I'd always known I'd see one day but now that the moment was here I was not sure I wanted to look.

But I asked another question, stepping closer into the details I had to know, "Who did it?"

"Now just who that was who made the motions, I don't recall," Bill said.

"And was my mother there in the room when the actual

vote took place or did they ask her to step outside?" I asked, certain that my mother must have had that detail wrong when she remembered sitting among her church members and watching them lift their hands around her.

"Oh yes," Cindi said. "They wouldn't ask her to step out. It was public record. She would have been right there when it happened."

And my mother, who has had no memory of that night—though I had asked her about it from one hundred different angles—rubbed her hands slowly together, lifted her head, and said quietly, looking right at me, "Barbara Randall made the motion and Mary Hovey seconded it."

"You remember?" I asked, confused that the names had finally come to her.

"I see them," she said, and shook her head, her mouth tight with an expression of toughness I've seen before. There is a certain bravado that has helped my mother endure what people are capable of doing to each other—she wore it now. She had remembered.

Two ordinary people took our church from us. Two women. Who drank tea in our kitchen. Whom I still meet sometimes at the post office or the October Fair. Women I know.

I looked around the room. Cindi, Bill, and my mother were all talking at once, relieved to have found the answer for me. Remembering the night.

I wanted to go lie down for a while in the bedroom, under a big pile of blankets and feel across my face an icy stream of frozen air from the crack in the window. The answer hadn't helped after all.

I had always imagined strangers. Not people I knew. Maybe some couple had voted out my mother without really knowing her. People who had lived in our town a short while and had long since moved on.

I lived in a small place where everyone who saw me ride by on my new two-wheeler knew my name. Knew I was June and Dick Young's daughter. And Peter and Richie Young's sister.

But we had to be taught that not everyone was safe. That there were strangers who could drive right into our town when no one was paying attention. It had happened to a little girl in Indiana. It could happen here. Strangers took you. They didn't care that you belonged to your family, that you loved the roads of your town, and the people you saw each day. They wanted to take you from it.

And it was strangers I imagined who had taken the church from my family. But women I know? This was so very, very much more complicated.

I looked up, refocusing on the conversation going on around me. Cindi and Bill and my mother had moved on. They were laughing together, looking to me to join them.

I listened to their conversation about the farm: the water pipes that always froze, the burro that was forever blocking the way of the school bus, the day Cindi drove the tractor into the side of the barn. I laughed at the stories, though I've heard them before. Laughing at these other times seemed to mean that not everything had been taken from us. We all seemed to need that.

After our friends left, I cleaned up the dishes and gave my mother a goodnight kiss. We didn't say much. It had been good to be with our friends again. But it was hard to find the words to put to the rest of it.

I let the dogs out for one last run, and found my way, exhausted, into bed under a pile of old blankets that smelled like years of cigarettes and mothballs. Eventually, I slept.

A few days later, it was New Year's Eve. My mother and I had not really talked about the visit with Cindi and Bill. I was still trying to figure out what it meant to me. Maybe she was too.

By late afternoon, I was groggy from a day of reading and napping. I walked down the snowy road to the landing to clear my head. Instead of turning back when I got to the edge of the pond, I walked out onto the ice, windblown with crusts of snow.

As I made my way down the pond, I saw two children out by the island, pulling sleds, slowly making their way toward me and the shore. I was glad they were heading back. It gets dark so suddenly when it gets dark here. As we got closer to each other, though, I saw that they were not children at all but small men, bundled in layers and layers of flannel shirts and stretched out sweaters. Their heavy wool trousers were tucked into ancient leather boots, giving them the look of gnomes. I called hello but they seemed hesitant in their approach.

I wondered if I looked threatening in my big red jacket, all wound up in my scarf with my hat pulled low, stomping heavily so I didn't slip and fall.

I called hello again. We were all so bundled perhaps they didn't hear me. One passed me and smiled politely. I saw from the piled-up assortment in his pull sled that they had been ice-fishing. Once he was safely past me, he said, "Pretty evening," and pointed to the bright curve of the waxing moon and the exclamation of Venus just above it.

"Venus looks beautiful," I said and we both stood looking up at it.

"It's a satellite," he said, quietly, after a bit. "Japanese. Russian."

"Really?" I asked, questioning readily what I knew to

be true, always one to give in too quickly to the authoritative voice.

His friend approached and he said, "No, no, Walter, that's Venus. A planet. It's okay." He spoke gently to his friend with much intent on reassurance. He turned to me and said softly, "Walter escaped from Poland. The rest of his family was killed. He gets confused." He nodded to me knowingly. "They are old worries."

I nodded back sadly and smiled at Walter to show I could be trusted. I asked about the noise we heard. A sound like a low, thrumming drum. *Bwrronng. Bwrronng.* A deep sound that scared me. Under the ice, under the water. Under the world.

"Do you think it's okay for me to walk to the other end?" I asked, never really trusting myself to the reliability of the ice of ponds and lakes.

"Oh, this is just right for a good walk. At least twelve inches thick," the friend told me, and I believed him, having always thought that ice fishermen know a little bit more about life than the rest of us.

"To the uninitiated that sound means danger, but actually it is the ice expanding, making room. Sometimes you'll see it send a crack right across in front of you and you'll think you're done for sure. But that crack's making room for more ice."

I tucked this information away for possible future use, wondering if I would ever believe it if it happened. My feet were cold standing in one place, so I stomped them and clapped my hands.

"Yes, it's getting dark. We should all go home," the friend announced. "Let's go, Walter. Careful there on that bare patch of ice."

I said, "Happy New Year to you both," shyly, unable to think of another way to mark an end to the encounter. I turned down the pond, listening for the deep drum sound of the old pond and its winter work.

"2001, Walter!" I heard the friend remark as they walked away. "Did you ever think we'd see it?"

He chuckled, and I smiled at their exchange. I looked down for where to take my next step across the expanding ice, and headed toward home and the new things I had learned.

# CHAPTER SEVENTEEN

# Bob's Transmission

I HAD JUST SPENT over a thousand bucks on my van and the transmission was still slipping. It was a rainy morning and I had a hundred things to accomplish after I dropped the girls off at school. But instead, I had to drive through all the slow, rain-puddled traffic, back to the transmission shop.

Now I am basically a reasonable person. I tried not to be nasty about it. But I did insist that the owner come for a drive with me to listen to the peculiar drone in the engine.

We ran from his shop to my van. It was really pouring. I got into the passenger's side and watched as he started the engine, adjusted the seats, the mirrors, and the wipers to just the right speed. A careful driver, this Bob. He turned off my music and listened. Revved the engine. Shrugged. We pulled out of the parking lot and out onto a back street, scattered with small, dark barrooms and dingy grocery stores.

We drove for a while in silence, not hearing the noises that I had been hearing all morning. All we could hear was the rain pounding on the roof and slipping around the tires. "It doesn't seem to be doing it now," I said guiltily.

"That's usually the way it goes," he said with a friendlier smile than I expected. He drove a few more blocks and then pulled into an ice-cream stand to turn around. "So, what do you do for work?" he asked me, waiting for his turn to pull out onto the busy street.

"I'm a writer," I said, always a little uncomfortable saying such a thing to a guy like him.

"It's really great work," I added, defensively.

"If you can make any money at it," he said and turned to look at me in question.

"Yah, well I'm making some money," I said and hoped he wouldn't ask how much. If you calculate it hourly, over a lifetime, it doesn't work out so great.

"So what do you write about?"

"I'm writing a book about who gets to decide who belongs to God and who doesn't," I explained. "It's based on some stuff that happened when I was a girl." I told him a brief version of the story, not really sure how much he wanted to hear. When he took the beauty salon lady out to test drive her car, did he listen to intricate details of the vast variety of perms available today? Did he hear about the complicated steps that guarantee a really good highlight?

But he listened. With convincing interest. "That's a lousy thing," he said. "I can't figure it out, you know? I went all Catholic growing up—parochial, high school, masses, holy days—the whole bit. But mostly I remember mean nuns. Some of them were real sickos."

"You hear a lot of that," I said, wondering why that was so.

He shrugged and revved the engine again trying to listen for anything suspicious.

"I'll tell you a God story," he said and turned up the speed of the wipers. "This one will make you puke." He explained how his best friend had died a few years ago. He had gotten involved with drugs. Drank too much. That kind of thing.

In the last months of his life, my transmission guy spent a lot of time with his best friend. He wasn't trying to change his habits ("There is nothing anyone can do when a guy doesn't wanna stop."), but he was there with him to wait it out.

Sometimes they'd get a few six-packs and hang out at the friend's mother's house. She had a big screen TV and a room full of recliners. They had a lot of laughs.

But then the friend's sister started getting religious. "I mean, we'd walk in and there she would be with all these people sitting around the table *reading the Bible*."

He said the words like I would never be able to believe such a thing was possible. "We used to walk by her and that table full of Bible-thumpers and just laugh." He shook his head, tapping the steering wheel with his grease-lined fingernails. "She used to be the biggest partier of all. What a friggin' hypocrite."

"Did it seem to make any difference in her?" I asked, always curious about such things.

"The only difference I could see was that she was always reading that stupid Bible of hers. I just couldn't believe it." He shook his head, wiping off my dashboard with his hand. It actually didn't need to be wiped, but I let it go.

"Did your friend die?" I asked, getting him to continue the story.

"Yah, three years ago. He was just too far gone. Couldn't moderate it, you know what I'm saying? I love to drink, but I know how to stop while it still feels good."

I nodded and offered him half of the bagel I had bought on the way over. He shook his head and patted his belly. I wasn't sure that half a wheat bagel was what was causing the belly issue for our Bob, but didn't say so. I was more interested in his story.

"So what happened?" I asked, swallowing a mouthful of what turned out to be a rather disappointing bagel.

"The thing was, she didn't even help him. His own friggin' sister. My buddy was really suffering and she would just sit there . . . reading!" He looked at me so long and so intently I thought we were going to end up wrapped around a telephone pole. "What kind of religion is that?"

I shook my head. I am no longer willing to take responsibility for every Christian who has ever lived.

"And then she went off to live in Florida to become a minister or something. That took the cake—a minister!" He sputtered. "So, what? Does everybody get to be a minister when you're a Protestant?"

I said I wasn't sure. The process seemed to be different depending on the denomination.

"Yah, well I don't get all that denominations stuff. With a priest, at least they have to go through a million years of school. And then . . . well, you know what I mean. The vows and stuff. They have to really want it, is what I'm saying."

I wasn't prepared to get into a discussion about the pros and cons of celibacy with my transmission guy. I was starting to get the feeling that his questions were beyond the realm of our present situation.

"So then what?" I asked. By this time we were just driving around, not really paying attention to the engine or its absent drone.

"What happened was the mother got really sick too. It was awful for the family. All that at once," he said. He beeped the horn at the car in front of us. Its driver had had the nerve to wait for three seconds at the green light before accelerating.

"And that idiot didn't even come home to help her. I mean, the mother was *really* sick. She needed her daughter, but her lousy daughter was too busy becoming a minister to come home. What do you think of that?"

"I don't know . . . I guess I thought people can misrepresent God," I said. "It happens a lot. And then we get mad at God."

"What do you mean?" he asked. "If we can't trust church people to represent God, who do we?"

Such a good question, I think to myself. But instead I said, "I know what you're saying. But listen," I started to talk with my hands, as if their additional emphasis would get my point through to him more clearly. "The church isn't God. The Catholic church isn't. The Protestant church isn't. No religion. They are interpretations of God."

We stopped at a red light and he turned and looked right at me like I might be on to something. I continued, "They aren't God. That's the thing we have to remember. I spend a lot of time trying to distinguish between the two. I find it a lot of work. Real tricky."

We pulled back into the lot of his shop and he put the van in park. It was raining hard but he rolled the window down a little to let in some air.

"The church isn't God," he said slowly.

"No, and that sister isn't God. Really, I'm sure of that one."

"She didn't even help her own mother."

I nodded. "That kind of thing is hard to take."

He gripped the steering wheel and turned it this way and that as he sat there thinking. "You mean it's like my transmission shop?"

I didn't know what he meant.

"I mean you're looking at this building and these signs and the lifts and all. You think that's Bob's Transmission. But it isn't. Bob's Transmission is in here," he pointed to his head. "It's me and what I know about cars."

He turned the wipers down. The rain was finally letting up. "And maybe you bring your car to me and some idiot guy who works for me takes it out for a drive and tells you there is nothing wrong with it and two days later it's wrecked. Because some jerk said he was Bob's Transmission. But he wasn't. He was just a dumb frig who didn't know what he was doing."

I laughed hard. "That's what I'm saying."

He laughed too. "And then you never come back again because you think *that's* what Bob's Transmission is all about. Is that how you think it is with God?"

"Bob," I said, "that's *exactly* how I think it is with God."

He drummed his fingers on the steering wheel some more, looking up at his building, looking up at the sky. "Well, I better get back in there," he said. "They're gonna think we're doing something in here."

"We don't want *that*," I said and laughed as I went around to the driver's side.

"Bring the van back on a day when it's not raining," he said. "It's too hard to check anything when the engine is all wet."

He ran toward the door of the shop, his jacket pulled up over his head. "Make sure you ask for me when you bring it back," he called as he pulled open the door and stepped inside. I watched through my fogged up window, as he shook off his jacket, hung it on a hook beneath a motor oil sign, and reached for a Styrofoam cup of coffee. Then I drove away.

# CHAPTER EIGHTEEN

# The River
# of Loss

MY FATHER BAPTIZED ALTHEA PERKINS, aged seventy-eight, in early June of 1965. He was wearing his good suit. He had taken his jacket off, and laid it on a fallen log at the edge of the water where the good people of The First Church of God had gathered to watch the old sinner cleansed whiter than snow.

The starched sleeves of his Sunday shirt were rolled up and his arms looked stronger than they really were.

He held Althea, whose new dress from Hovey's floated up around her loose and shiny like oil on water. And he, my Dad, (John the Baptist, Jesus himself—what difference was there to me?) called out in his deep voice, "Althea Perkins, I baptize you in the name of the Father, and the Son, and the Holy Spirit." He eased the old woman back into the cold water as if they were dancing.

We, on the shore, had witnessed such scenes a hundred times before. The newest member of the fold standing waist deep in water, stained, laden with old ways. But then came the moment, the baptism, the immersion itself, just as Jesus showed us. Letting go of the former. The promise of the new.

He held her under a moment, and then pulled her up. Imagining holy deliverance, we looked into her eyes to see for ourselves the great things God can do.

But a dazed expression flushed her face. And then we all heard her words—there was no hiding it—when she stood, caught her breath, and shouted, "*Jee-sus Chri-iist*, was that cold!"

I wonder now if it *worked*, that particular baptism? You go under; you come up changed, set for eternity. But did she become one of God's people that day? Does she get to belong, even though her first act as the newly baptized was to use the name of Jesus in a way you just don't?

I do not know how it goes with God. Which ways work and which ways don't. I can never quite trust those easy formulas people come up with for who gets to belong and who doesn't.

I do know what my father and mother taught me: conversations we had over the years, lines from the Bible, from favorite hymns.

And I know what I learned from the people they chose as their friends. People from my town. Who never went to church. Who didn't seem to speak of God. Who didn't use the language of denomination, those code words that let others know you were *in*.

I was confused, though. These friends of ours did not call themselves the people of God but they were always *doing* the things God said to do: sharing what they had with those in need; not picking up the first quick stone of judgment; offering help but never needing for anyone else to know about it. They loved us, their neighbors, as themselves. Better even.

But now they are being taken from me. One, and then

another. The people I belonged to in my hometown are dying off. Every year I watch another of them go.

I want some reassurance that they matter to God. That their versions of being the people of God are versions that also count. I am holding Jesus to His words, "You will know them by their fruits."

I need to believe that the kindnesses Tessie and Dick Wakefield showed us in a hundred ways are like that fruit God says we will recognize. I want some reassurance, in exchange for letting go of them, those kind neighbors my mother could count on when she missed her mother so badly she would cry all afternoon.

My mother had just eloped after knowing my father only a few months. She had left her mother all those miles behind. Her nine brothers and one sister. That assortment of aunts and uncles and cousins who so crowded the big old house that my mother slept together with her mother and sister in the same bed until the night she drove away and eloped with Dick Young.

Tessie and Dick, who lived right next door, understood their role. They invited her over for a cup of tea, and opened that old farmhouse door every time my mother knocked.

Years later, my mother still went to sit at Tessie and Dick's kitchen table when she was lonesome. She held me in her lap, sipped her tea, took a drag from her cigarette, and cried about the lack of money for a car that worked, or the way my father listened in on his CB radio all night and didn't give her a hand with the kids or the house.

And Tessie—years older than my mother, and long beyond the days of young children and errant husbands—remembered the sort of pain that clouded my mother's eyes. She shook her head in understanding, reached for a doughnut from the wide brimmed jar, and set it on a napkin in front of the young woman she loved like a daughter.

Tessie made those home-fried doughnuts on Mondays and Fridays. They were heavy and not too sweet, the kind that left a circle of grease on your paper napkin, soaking it from white to translucent gray. Then on Tuesdays, she pulled her roller washing machine in from the shed to wash the tan chino shirts and pants Dick always wore.

Dick had his own routines. He kept several packs of playing cards going at one time, working them to just the right point of broken in for his ongoing games of solitaire. I remember standing next to him, watching him position the colorful queens and stark aces, and once I patted the soft white whiskers on his cheek.

He drove a truck. He hunted. He always got his deer. He was gentle though, and one time he told me that he'd have to cut off my thumb with his hunting knife, if I didn't stop sucking it. But I didn't for one moment feel afraid of him.

Here's what I can hold on to: the memory of their cluttered, welcoming table. The lazy Susan in the middle of it with three pepper shakers, one salt, a stack of bills, a sugar box with a broken lid, three foil packets of ketchup from a takeout dinner two weeks ago, a cup of assorted pens, a pad of paper from the Meredith Village Savings Bank, and a jar of mustard with not much left in it.

I hold on to the memory of a smelly fishing creel and a tangle of poles by the front door. The suggestion that the fish were always biting. And the tall stacks of *National Geographic* magazines in which I first saw a world other than my hometown. Hours spent at their crowded kitchen table, learning life. That's what is left for me.

What's not left is the people themselves. Not Dick. Nor Tessie, who smoked Camel cigarettes, no filters, that left her voice husky in a way that was tougher than she was. I remember her as a sturdy woman, though. Sturdy and strong. Reliable.

So it did not completely surprise me when the night before my husband and I were bringing home our firstborn child from the hospital, I dreamt about Tessie.

I dreamt that Roy was picking me up at the front door of the hospital and I didn't want to get in the car with him. I was holding Elizabeth, our first daughter, and I didn't trust him. I feared that, like many first-time dads, he wasn't quite ready for what it would take.

And in the dream, Tessie appeared in the seat next to him. She had been dead for years by then and I had forgotten her face, but that night I saw her again so clearly. She sat in the front seat right next to my husband. I told her my worries with my eyes, as I stood holding my baby.

She told me to get in with him. I heard her voice, its familiar, husky comfort, "It's okay, get in the car. He'll come around good."

And I was right. Roy wasn't ready to be a father yet. And Tessie was right. He came around good.

I do not want to let these people go, though the river swept them away from me years ago. There are things I've left unsaid. Things I want to say now. Like how grateful I am to them for knowing what my young mother needed when she was a young wife. And for showing up in a dream to help me when I, too, had a new baby and a young husband in a place miles from my mother.

And I didn't want to let go of Aaron Foster; that man who never said more than a few sentences to me my whole life, but whose quiet ways I have not forgotten.

He pulled up each morning in his rusted green pickup to feed and water the cow he kept in our barn, and came back each night regardless of the weather or the condition of his tires.

His wife came with him, though she never got out. She sat in the truck, her hair unbrushed, shoulders hunched, while Aaron scooped the grain and shoveled the stall. I waved to him and he would nod. But I avoided her because there was a look in her eyes that scared me.

Once, when I didn't see her for several days, and my father took to watering Aaron's cow, I asked him what had happened.

My father said, "He had to put her in Concord," which we all understood.

I nodded, silently, fiddling with the hasp on a stall door.

"It'd be nice if you said something to him," he said as he buttoned up his jacket and headed for the house.

I knew Aaron in this way: we were often in the barn at the same time, each doing our chores in silence.

And I had watched him, one cold morning before the sun came up, pull a wet calf from its heaving mother. My father woke us kids before dawn to go out with him to the cold barn and watch. Aaron had one barn boot against the cow's hind end, and one arm shoved up inside the swollen rim of her, to pull and pull at the slippery calf stuck inside.

It was an embarrassment for a ten-year-old girl, to see the old farmer's arm disappear into that massive hole. But I knew it was his kindness that made him do it. I knew because I watched the fear-filled clouds of breath come from that cow's nostrils with each contraction. And I saw the relief in that mother cow's eyes as she heaved one last, exhausted push, and Aaron pulled with all his weight, and the calf slipped out onto the hay in the dim barn light.

My Dad looked at us kids and said, "You'll never forget this. Ever." Then he smiled at my brother and me.

Aaron and I had stood together some afternoons, at the same water spigot, waiting for a pail to fill. When you are with someone you already know isn't going to talk, the silence doesn't bother you. It's even good. No words. Just the sound of water rushing into an empty tin bucket. A barn swallow swooping down. Or a cow shifting its weight on an old barn floor.

But my father wanted me to say something to Aaron about his wife's trouble. When it wasn't our way to talk, what could I say to a man who only nodded? Or who sometimes moved his mouth in a way that might be mistaken for a smile.

Lacking words, I made fudge for him, wrapped it in waxed paper with two rubber bands, and left it on the feed barrel.

He came that afternoon to do his chores, and almost left as usual. I watched him start to go. But as he was driving away he slowed, rolled down the window of his truck, and leaned out. "That fudge was good," he said.

I think it was our longest conversation ever. Young girl. Quiet farmer. Aaron Foster, first midwife of that first birth I ever witnessed. A birth that, just as my father knew, I have never forgotten. Nor ever stopped being grateful I had seen.

When cancer finally got Aaron, I stood on the shore of loss. People like that don't get replaced.

And I didn't want to lose Hazel Straw. I want to see her standing again on the caving front porch of her old house around the corner, on her thick, sure legs, looking out at Route 109 with one of her tamed raccoons in those big arms of hers. Raccoons, my father told me, that lived right in the old house with her. And when he told me this, it was with admiration not disdain. I think she and my father understood each other.

I want to be walking past, and hear her calling my name from her front porch. And she would be asking, as she always did, "How's your father doing? He eating his peanut butter?" and laugh her big old laugh, saying she never knew a man who liked peanut butter as much as Dick Young.

She was also our school cook, Hazel Straw, the one who served food that was either perfectly salty or perfectly sweet— all of it homemade in the huge black school stoves that gave off all that wonderful heat in the middle of winter. All of it made by Hazel who was faithful to serve it to us at the same time each day, no matter what.

Maybe it could be Friday, just one more time, when it was my turn to help her in the kitchen at Moultonboro Central School. Being with her in the school kitchen gave me the comfort of being home because she smoked my Dad's brand, and her smoking always made the kitchen smell like him. And she always gave my brother, Peter, an extra scoop of mashed potatoes when he came by in the lunchroom line, because she understood he didn't have the easiest time of it.

I appreciated the way Hazel Straw felt familiar when I had to be away from home during those long school hours. Hours when anything could happen.

Maybe I could watch her again as she pulled hot pans of fish sticks out of the big black ovens while calling out to me to cut the sheet cakes in even squares ("We don't need those fresh sixth grade boys fighting over who's got the bigger piece, now do we, Kathy?"). And I could look at her with her white apron stretched across her middle. I'd see it stained with grease from the government-issued potato puffs, and frayed at the hem from too many washings.

The schoolkids would collect their lunches on melamine-speckled trays with little compartments. Trays that were organized. Durable. That held warm, soft food. Food that helped us because it was given by someone who cared about us no matter who we were.

If I could see all this, now more clearly than I did back then, maybe I could understand, better, how when you lose someone you don't lose all of them. That what they gave you stays with you, no matter how strong the current of the river trying to pull them away.

I'm thinking all this and it's got me missing a woman who's been dead for years, who gave me all the attention I needed in a lunchroom kitchen whenever I had something to say. Some of what I'm left with is this simple. A taste for fish sticks and government-issued potato puffs, and the particular ways of a woman who tamed raccoons in a run-down house.

And now I have heard that Cecil Rivers may not regain consciousness. Oh, river, let him be.

He was coming home from a dance last Saturday night, where he plays the spoons and teaches country line dancing. They say he had a stroke and smashed his car into an old maple on Route 25.

"What a good way to go, though," Roy said when I told him the news from my hometown. "Eighty-six years old. A good night of dancing. . . ."

I suppose. Maybe eighty-six years is enough for Cecil.

But I will miss the loyalty he held for my father's memory. I will miss that every time I ran into him he would tell me how he missed my Dad.

Cecil had owned a woodshop uptown and he created a job there for my father when he was laid off and unemployed for six months. He provided a reason for my Dad to get up every day, and gave him the gift of working intently with his hands when that mind felt so bad.

Cecil was an expert fly fisherman, as well. People came

from all around the United States to our little town to buy the colorful flies he was famous for. He crafted the tiny bits of feathers and thin strings around shiny hooks, and laid them out in glass-covered cases, like diamonds.

Cecil Rivers. The size of a twelve-year-old boy. But not young-muscled like that. More like a chicken, stewed and tough.

The last time I saw Cecil was outside the Poultry House at the Sandwich Fair. I had just seen a blue-ribbon Rhode Island Red that had caused me to question the choices I have made in my life.

*Am I sure I want to live in a house where I can't have chickens?*

I walked out into the bright October sun and saw Cecil standing by the small, Ecuadorian flute players, smiling. We had never had Ecuadorian flute players at the Sandwich Fair before and I was interested to see Cecil nod his head just so to the bouncy music.

I walked right up to him and bent to give him a kiss on his leathery cheek. I don't hug Cecil. I always kiss him. I worry about his face getting lost in my generous bosom. Also, I've always thought of him as bigger than me, and I prefer to keep that illusion going.

"God, Kathy, you're just as pretty as ever," he said smiling up at me. This is one of the reasons I love him. He does not notice change.

"And how 'bout that Massachusetts fella? Is he treating you the way I would?"

I smiled and pointed to Roy and the girls who were just coming out of the chicken house. They had been detained at the "free bunnies to a good home" cage.

Cecil shook Roy's hand, laughing right out loud at how much the girls reminded him of me, thirty years ago. He told us about his dances, and all his girlfriends, and he showed us his new belt buckle, almost as big as he was. He invited us all over to his house and we promised, as we always do, that we would stop by.

Then we went off to get some hot apple pie and he left to watch the sheep show. And I was thinking, as I watched him walk away, maybe this time I would take the girls over to visit this man who was so good to my father at a time when kindheartedness was what he needed.

But he crashed into an old maple on Route 25 last Saturday night and they don't expect him to regain consciousness. Let go, let go. The river is running fast. I stand at its ruthless edge, watching it sweep past with the ones I've cared for most in this life.

I've been baptized in their loss. So will I see them again? Will it be like the Fourth of July barbecue after the parade down at the Lion's Club field? I like a picnic. I love a reunion. But just who is the reunion for?

I never saw Cecil go to church or heard him mention God. Or Aaron or Hazel. Or Tessie or Dick either. So what does that mean?

I don't know. I don't know. What I was taught doesn't fit with what I've seen.

Baptism. People of God. I stand on the shore of the river of loss, worrying who else will be taken from me. I try each time to find my way back. But there is no way back. The river carries me to an entirely different place.

I just want to know how it all turns out. But I only know what I know.

And, God, I have loved this life. When the time comes to let go again—all right, yes, I have done it before. I can do it again. I will let go.

I will stand at that cold water and watch them go. But, Jesus. Christ. I don't want to.

CHAPTER NINETEEN

# *The*
# *Present*

TALL LEADED GLASS WINDOWS lightened the room. My daughters, ages ten and six, sat in the children's worship center of our church on little rugs that circled a child-sized altar. When everyone had found a place to sit, the toddlers climbing comfortably into the older kids' laps, the storyteller slowly lit a candle and offered a quiet prayer.

The children watched as the storyteller stood, walked calmly to the parable shelves and removed a box, painted gold. She came back to her rug and sat. "A parable is a lot like a present. It has been given to us," she said, running her hand along its sides and top. "And sometimes parables seem to have lids on them. We need to get the lids off so we can see what might be inside."

She lifted the cover from the box and pulled out a wide piece of cloth, which she shook out and smoothed on the floor in front of her. "Sometimes the meaning of the gift seems hidden," she said, then removed a small container and placed it on the cloth. The children all leaned forward for a better view.

"Seeds," she said, opening the container and gently pressing her finger inside. "Mustard seeds." She looked up at the children and smiled.

"Once there was someone who said such amazing things, and did such wonderful things, that people began to follow him. As they followed, he told them about a kingdom: but they did not understand. They had never been to such a place. And they didn't know anyone who had. They didn't even know where it was. So one day they simply had to ask him, 'What is the kingdom like?'

"And he said, 'The Kingdom of Heaven is like a grain of mustard seed . . .'"

The storyteller placed a tiny seed into the open palm of each child. An ancient story was told again.

At coffee hour after the service, Elizabeth came hurrying in and showed me her hand. "Look," she said holding it right up near my face. I was looking for an injury of some sort but couldn't see the problem.

"No," she said, pointing to a tiny little fleck on her palm. "It's a mustard seed! See?"

"Oh," I said and smiled, knowing they had just heard one of my favorite Jesus stories. "Why do you have a mustard seed?"

"Jesus said it's like the kingdom of heaven," Jennie said, always quick to try to provide the answer before her older sister.

"Do *you* think it is?" I asked, trying to get beyond the quick answers. I try to let my daughters know that I wonder too about how a mustard seed could represent the kingdom of heaven. That questions like that last your whole life. And it is a good thing to live alongside them.

"The seed grows into a big tree that gives the birds a place to build their nests and gives shade to people who are hot from too much sun," Elizabeth said, and I heard the storyteller's words in her mouth. Then she added her own thoughts, "But it's so *tiny*. . . ."

I nodded, wanting to explain what was important to me about this parable. I wanted to say, *Listen to me girls. This is an important one: if you have just this tiny amount of faith—God will honor it and help grow it into something that will sustain you. Always. A place of rest for you, a place from which to grow. The source of everything you truly need. That one little speck.*

That is what I wanted to say.

But I didn't. Having been trained in the particular ways of this kind of storytelling, I said, slowly, "I wonder, too," trusting that they are better off discovering for themselves without my astounding knowledge.

There was much concern on the car ride home about how to keep that mustard seed from getting itself lost. We could barely see it, let alone keep track of it. When we got home, Elizabeth put it into a tiny box where she kept special things on her bureau and came down to the kitchen looking for lunch.

I was cutting up bunches of grapes for the plates of turkey and cheese sandwiches I was making. The girls stood around me, hungry and reaching for snacks.

"When I was a little girl, we were given a mustard seed necklace when we memorized the names of the books in the New Testament," I said, the memory coming back unexpectedly.

"Do you still have it?" Jennie asked.

"Well, actually, I never got it," I said, pouring them each a glass of milk.

"But you know the books of the New Testament," Elizabeth said. "You taught us that song."

"I do know the books of the New Testament," I said. "But I didn't get the necklace. It's a long story. I'll tell you when you are older."

The girls do not like to be told they are not old enough for a particular story. They protested. They like to think of themselves as ready for any truth. But I know better.

So, instead of continuing the conversation, I called Roy in from watering the garden and we all sat down to our sandwiches. I wished, as I often do, that we were the kind of family who had a huge Sunday dinner with meat and potatoes and gravy, served on the good china in the dining room, surrounded by church friends. The reality is we are more of a paper-plate-lunch-after-church-kind-of-family. But in my mind we are always just a week away from that homey hospitality.

After lunch, Roy asked Jennie to go with him to do a couple of errands. She likes to be his able assistant and he likes her cheery company. I was working my way toward my Sunday afternoon nap.

While I was reading in bed, Elizabeth came in and lay down beside me, something she doesn't normally do lest I try to convince her of the wonderfulness of napping. "Am *I* old enough to know why you didn't get the necklace?" she asked.

I looked at my daughter. Thought about myself at ten years old, trying to remember who I was then and what I needed. Trying to discern what she needed now.

"Yes, you are," I said slowly, considering what I wanted to tell her. I said what I thought would encourage my gentle girl. "I can tell *you*. I just didn't want to tell Jennie because it would make her sad."

"Will *I* feel sad?" she asked.

"I think you will feel compassion," I said. "And that's an important feeling. It was something that happened to my family, your Mamoo and Papa," I said using her names for my parents.

I told her about how my father was often ill when I was growing up, something she didn't know. That her Uncle Peter was a year younger than she is now. That I was only five and Uncle Richie had just been born. My father had to be put in the hospital for a long time. I explained that we didn't have enough money and so my mother had to get a job as a waitress. People at our church said it broke the rules for my mother to serve people drinks before their dinner.

"But Mamoo doesn't drink," Elizabeth argued.

My ten-year-old girl understood the distinction: why couldn't they?

"I know. It's really too bad they didn't think more about that," I said. "So what happened was, my family had to stop going to our church. So that's why I didn't get the necklace."

"That *is* too sad for Jennie," she said, more comfortable with her little sister's emotions than her own. Then she looked over at me resting on a pile of pillows. "Did they say sorry?"

I shook my head. "You know, Elizabeth, I don't think they realized what they were doing. How it would hurt our lives. I really believe they thought they were doing the right thing." I gave her shoulder a squeeze as if to relieve some of what she was feeling. "We all make mistakes, Lizzie. Especially about God."

"But we are supposed to *love each other*," she said, her voice filling with that innocent self-righteousness ten year olds are so good at.

"You're right," I said. "But you know, I think it is like parables and that mustard seed. There are a lot of different ways to think about the things God says. We get mixed up."

She looked skeptical. She had not yet run into any complications with her love for God. We took her to church each week where she heard yet another story about how much God loves her. Where people smiled when they saw our cute little family walk in the door. She saw her parents loving God. It had not yet occurred to her that our love for God might include its share of complications: struggles with church and people and beliefs. That there were times when we didn't know what to make of it all. That sometimes it seemed a blind, darned faith that got us to the next day.

She did not know that so much of life is like a parable box with a lid you are trying to uncover. But I had said enough for one day. The conversation tired my mind more than I would have expected. So I gave her a hug and said, "So show some love for your mother and let me get a nap before your Dad and Jennie come bouncing back in."

A few months later, I encountered another parable. It happened unexpectedly—layered with new meaning from old, familiar images, just as parables do. We were in Washington, D.C., visiting my brother Peter and his partner, Rob, for Thanksgiving. We had not yet been to visit them in their new townhouse and were grateful for the long weekend together.

We spent long days touring the museums and monuments, followed by elaborate and delicious meals they prepared for us each night. Everyone got to do what he or she most wanted. Roy wanted to take the White House tour. Elizabeth wanted to see the Vietnam Memorial. Jennie wanted to climb up and down the stairs of the Lincoln Memorial.

So we toured the blue room and the yellow room and the red room of the White House. We walked the somber lines of The Wall and I held the girls up so they could trace their fingers over the name of Ding and Leanie's son, Steven W. Martin. We watched, exhausted, as Jennie jumped up and down the stairs of the Lincoln Memorial about a hundred times.

What I had most wanted to do was to visit the National Cathedral. Although we had been to visit in D.C. several times before, I had never been able to take the time to explore it. It was a place Rob knew well and thought I would love. He showed me photographs of some of the stained glass windows and chapels. He told the girls about the window with a real piece of the moon right in it. We made a plan to go for Thanksgiving services and leave time to tour the art and architecture after the Mass.

The cathedral was larger than I had imagined. I read from the small tour book I bought at the door, "Entering the Gothic cathedral, the worshiper confronts the mysteries of faith. The soaring architecture and embellishments direct the spirit of humankind upward toward God." I looked up and around at the stained glass windows. They were not dark and subdued, closing us in, but bright and brilliant with swirls of color that floated high above our searching eyes.

We each wandered, separately, quietly, discovering something new and beautiful at every turn. When it was time for the service to begin we walked toward a chapel decorated with all different kinds and shapes of fresh breads. Bread of earth. Bread of heaven. All in one.

The ushers greeted my husband and me, our daughters, my brother and his partner. Together, we recited the prayers for the day. Listened to the words of the Last Supper. Returned again to the altar for the bread and wine that restores us. We sang a plain and beautiful hymn. Received a blessing and watched as people hurried off to check on the stuffed turkeys cooking in their ovens back home.

We lingered. I wanted to find the little stone chapel I read about in my guidebook because it had a carving of my favorite parable. I was intent on finding it, though it took several attempts, down a long series of stairs and confusing turns.

But then I was upon it—one of my favorite images of God—the Good Shepherd holding the lamb. The renderings I had always seen depicted sturdy looking lambs slung over the rugged shoulders of some young shepherd boy who looked confidently at his viewer. The legs of the animal were always grasped as if it were a wiry and spunky little thing that might run off and get itself lost again at any moment.

But this carving was different. The shepherd held the lamb in his arms, looking tenderly down upon his charge. And the way its little legs hung, so all-in, so absolutely worn out—and yet wrapped in the able arms of the willing shepherd—brought a whole new meaning for me.

It didn't seem anymore that God was using this brawny strength to keep us from going where He didn't want us to go: it was that He is willing to come to us when we are so undone we cannot possibly find another step within us.

The parable was not about authority, but rather, tenderness.

I felt so calm there in that small chapel I didn't want ever to move again. But my brother came looking for me, telling me the others were ready to go. There was food to cook. A meal to celebrate together. I sighed and stood. We all joined up outside where we walked through herb gardens still heavy with scent in the November air.

The seasons changed. Thanksgiving to Christmas. Pentecost to Advent. The telling of parables circled along the church year to the story of the God-child's birth.

I tried to attend to the church's new season of preparing for the mystery of that night in Bethlehem. But who can find stillness in those weeks? Still, each year I try again.

We stayed up late for the Christmas Eve service. The choirboys' voices sang the experience, ". . . the thrill of hope, a weary world rejoices, for yonder dawns a new and glorious morn. . . ." Yes, we were weary. Yes, we needed the thrill of hope. We always do. We each held a candle, lit one to another, and lifted them against darkness, eventually filling the whole sanctuary with the gold light.

Then it was Christmas morning. Having welcomed the newborn king, it was time for that other, noisier part of the holiday: the presents.

The girls usually go right for their stockings—eager for the little surprises Roy collects for them all year—but we always make them wait until we light the logs in the fireplace and make a pot of coffee.

That morning, though, instead of rushing to her own gifts, Elizabeth brought a little box to me. Roy and Jennie watched and I could see they were up to something. I lifted the lid of the present, looked in, and then into the eyes of my girl.

"Do you like it?" Elizabeth asked, her face all excitement. Then she asked, "Is it too small?"

"No, it's perfect," I said, lifting a little gold chain with its glass bulb and floating mustard seed. "And I love that it is girl-sized. This is the necklace I wanted."

Elizabeth smiled at me, sure she had set things right. And Roy and I exchanged the kind of glance that parents sometimes do when their child has shown compassion.

"We got it at the cathedral," Jennie said, explaining their success. "And you didn't even see us do it!"

Though I tried the necklace to my throat, I preferred to hold the little glass bulb and seed. I thought if I looked closely enough, I might see what it had been waiting all these years to show me.

Elizabeth kept checking on me as the morning passed, her eyes catching mine. I tried to pay attention to the girls as they opened their gifts, but I kept imaging a conversation with God about the present—the reminder that a tiny bit of faith can keep you going.

I imagined Him wanting to say to me, *Listen, Kate. The way a mustard seed is like the kingdom of heaven is this: it takes a long time to find a place to grow well. But you are doing it. And now you help these daughters. Look at it all. I'm there.*

Am I just putting my words in God's mouth? That always worries me. Yet I want to pay attention to each layer of meaning as my own girl gives me the very thing I needed when I was a girl.

I see God in the timing and the circumstance and perfection of the present. I recognize the incredible reality: parables are more than stories once told. They speak of the newness of grace over and over again through all the ages. It's right there in my hand—a mustard seed necklace. Which is like the kingdom of heaven in ways I still don't understand. But that part doesn't matter so much to me. What matters is the hope I didn't know I still needed in this one, particular way.

# CHAPTER TWENTY

*Returning*

THE PATTERN OF THE HOURS I spend at our cabin in New Hampshire is this. Sun sets over Red Hill just after 9:00 P.M. in the summer. Within a half hour the bats begin to swoop. If they come close enough the rapid flap of their wings is a vibration to the ear. By 10:00 P.M., if you pay attention, you will see the occasional firefly in the wild blueberry.

One common loon calls each night just after 10:00 P.M., off the southern end of Emerson Island. If I am laughing hard in those moments when it calls goodnight, or maybe singing with my family, or if I've gone inside the cabin to grab a strike-anywhere match to get the campfire started, I miss the nightly loon call altogether.

The peepers commence—those insistent, hidden tree frogs—retelling the only story they know to tell. And also the bullfrogs that line the pond edge and gulp a drunken call from their chubby throats, like the low note plunks of my father's banjo. They won't shut up until after 2:00 A.M.

Then, right when I am about to fall asleep under layers of old quilts and flannel sheets there are sounds of an animal just outside my window. I used to be certain these frequent sounds—crack of branch, pinecone snap, foot and claws on stone wall—were sounds of bear. And I would wake, instantly. Ready to be torn apart.

I have now slept in our cabin on my parents' land for many nights of many years and I have learned to distinguish the lesser mammal (the weasels and coons whose work it is to explore the dark) from the greater (the deer who likes the wild blueberry, or the moose that stood just beyond the screen door, knee deep in pond marsh, one glorious morning just before light). I no longer startle at mammal sounds. Trusting the safety of the tiny cabin, the warm bed, I note the sounds, breathe in, and give myself to sleep.

By 3:00 A.M., night is night. Silent. Black on a moonless night. The woods and I sleep deeply until the mallards and purple finches awaken and begin their glory work again.

That's when you hear dawn before you see it. The sky is still too dark to make out the line of pine and birch on Emerson Island, or my kayak, which waits for me, tied with old rope to the creaky dock, a few feet away.

If the wind is just so you can feel mist rising from the pond, and smell the damp remains of last night's campfire.

Within minutes I am able to delineate pond and pine. Then pine and sky. The loon calls from the southern end of the island soon after 5:00 A.M. I always hear the morning loon call. There is nothing to interrupt it. It echoes down the pond, through the screens of our cabin where I lie somewhere between the need for the smell of sleep on the blankets that tangle me, and the need for hot coffee in a warm mug and a trip in my kayak, down the pond toward the sun rising over the Ossipee Range, through the pattern of sound and silence of which I am a faithful student.

I choose the kayak. A bass surfaces ten feet away. It flips up into the morning air for just a moment, the sun reflecting every color of its small perfection. I lay my paddle across my lap and rest to consider the spreading concentric circles it leaves as it swims away.

I lift my mug and sip comforting coffee I boiled on the camp stove; then recite a psalm, or a poem, or a list of thanks, adding my sound to the ones that have already been offered. For hours. For years. By birds and trees and every living thing at the edge of Lee Pond.

I turn back toward the camp and climb carefully from my kayak. A water snake slithers in the warm water near my feet but I am not afraid. Ding Martin taught me years ago that the snakes of Lee Pond are more afraid of me than I of them.

I walk slowly on wet, bare feet across pinchy ground cover toward our little place: the gathering of Adirondack chairs around the campfire, the cinder blocks we use as end tables or foot rests, and the old metal pail that we, good scouts, fill with pond water and keep at the ready just like Dad taught us.

At the center of this small scene is a gathering of rocks, formed in a circle beneath towering bull pines that drop sappy cones and dry needles and branches. Granite rocks. That's all you would think they are. A small ring of them with a few half-burned logs leaning against each other.

But they are not only rocks—those small chunks of New Hampshire granite—they are a symbol of the year I had to find a way past illness to be my daughters' mom again. From the summer I had spent presumably recovering from surgery.

"Come to New Hampshire," my mother had said to me. "The mountain air will make you well. Just like in *Heidi*."

So my good husband packed up our daughters. Packed up his wife, and drove us from the city to my family's land in the shadow of Red Hill.

But I didn't get better. Instead, I lost ground.

Weak—emptied of the life force I took for granted—unable to walk, without assistance, from the edge of the pond to the front door of my mother's house, a few hundred feet away. I—who had hiked steep mountains for the pleasure of the burn in my muscles and the tug of air into my heaving lungs—I couldn't walk without leaning on the shoulder of my own young child.

Hours. Long days. Weeks. I sat in an Adirondack chair, my head back, eyes closed, waiting for health to return. Despairing it would not.

Slowly and mysteriously my health had left me months before—months where at first I had simply thought I was too busy. Tired. Run down. But then I discovered the lump. Recognized the gravity of the constant sore throat. The continuous fever. The swollen lymph glands. But the tumor was benign. Why was I getting worse?

I watched my daughters set out in the canoe toward the big rock where they liked to swim: watched with the knowledge that if they needed help, there was nothing I could do. I could not paddle to them, swim to them, or walk on water, as I'm sure I would have done when I was well.

When you are long ill you can't remember anymore how you used to be.

Waking in the morning, hours after my family had started their day, I'd walk up to my mother's from the cabin for a little visit, trying to appear normal. I'd ask what everyone was doing and feign interest. Ability.

I know, too well, what it means to have a sick parent. What it is like to stand next to the bed where they are asleep yet again (will they sleep forever?). You speak to them, call them. But your young, needing voice does not reach them. They are lost to illness.

I know how that takes away a piece of trust you never get back. Was I now doing that to my children? Oh, God. Are you seeing this?

I would return to the cabin for another nap. Sometimes my mother would walk down to check on me. To wake me. Be sure I was still breathing. Sometimes she brought a cold cloth to wipe my face. Or she would lean over me, and take my drawn face in both of her beautiful, slender hands, as if pushing her life into me.

We would walk slowly up the path to her house and sit together on the porch. One day I told her what I couldn't tell anyone else. That I thought I was slowly dying. And my biggest fear was that my girls would not remember the mom I really was. The one I had been only last summer.

I was a mother who encouraged adventures, just as my father always had. Who urged them to swim all the way to Walker's Point—don't be afraid, you can do it—the very first day I thought were big enough. And when Jennie, at five, joined Elizabeth and me for her first swim out, she was too tired for the trip back. I was well then. The mother I wanted to be to my girls. So she climbed on my back, like a baby loon, and I, strong mother loon, swam her safely home.

But where was that mom I used to be? And who was this one who seemed to scare her very own children with her bleary eyes and shaky legs?

I adjusted myself in my chair where I sat near my mother, looking out at Red Hill. *I lift up my eyes unto the hills. From whence does my help come? My help comes from the Lord, who made heaven and earth.* But was there help for me? Really?

I believed God was aware of me and my despair. I was not so certain, though, He would intervene. Who is God in moments like these? And what should I ask for? Healing? Courage?

Did I dare risk my relationship with Him, the relationship I had struggled so hard to reclaim, by asking for anything at all?

Was it better not to ask? To avoid disappointment?

Because if God doesn't respond at a time like this, what does that mean about every darn thing I have allowed myself to believe?

I lowered my eyes from the familiar view beyond the porch and looked down at my hands. My body was starting to harden again. There was something wrong with my muscles. With my joints. I could not stay in one position for more than ten minutes or my neck and hands and legs would stiffen. Cement replaced blood.

I was losing the ability to move. To lift my arms to braid my girls' hair. To carry food. I dropped plates. Small ones.

The days at the pond were interspersed with trips to the city for appointments with specialists. Blood tests. More specialists. The row of prescription bottles by my bed grew.

My husband did everything. Took care of our girls. Of food and laundry and the million daily tasks we used to share. He kept his business strong. Researched for hours, at the end of long days, for possible reasons for my symptoms. He brought me little bouquets of flowers from our gardens for my bedside table. Stayed awake with me when I couldn't sleep.

We tried hard to get me back. Every way we could.

There were trips every other day to the health store for fruits and vegetables, vitamins and teas. I drank gallons of peculiar juices. Tested my hair, my toenails, my saliva, my pee. Anything that might give a clue to what had happened. Where had I *gone?*

Then one afternoon, back at the cabin, I was waking alone from another deep nap. Roy had taken the girls to our house in the city to visit their friends. To check on the gardens and the mail. To give me a few days without the pressure of guilt that their sad glances evoked in me.

I got the idea of a campfire. If all I could do was sit and stare, maybe I could turn that into something else. Something for me and my girls to do together. A campfire. It might be just the thing—my best shot at participating in their lives that summer. The only way I could think of.

So I carried rocks from the near woods, rocks the size of cantaloupes that the previous summer I could have hefted by the armload. But now I lugged one at a time. Rested. And considered, as I caught my breath, whether I could carry another.

I watched the strange days pass. Watched a good idea transform into hope. It was hope I had lost that now I was reclaiming. Why these changes happen, I cannot tell you. Is it prayer? Is it determination? Some important combination of both?

I only know that in this life I have witnessed, a few times, a moment when something hard gives, lets go, and a new way that seemed impossible becomes possible.

I was building a campfire for my girls. One rock at a time, I built a circle—my own monument to the decision to find a place somewhere between vibrant and ill. A place my father had not found. But that I was determined to.

It took a few days. This one, small thing. Roy and the girls were coming back soon and my project was not done. So I asked Richie and Ronda's children to help.

Benjamin, at six, was stronger than I that summer. And Emily, only four, could match my efforts. My brother's children. My god-children. I would show them this about God's grace: you don't always receive the clear answer, the miraculous solution—but you get a new way of looking at your life. And sometimes that is enough.

. . .

We had our first campfire that night when Roy, Elizabeth, and Jennie returned. Rich and Ronda walked over from their house on the other side of my parents' land. My mother, who preferred her screened in porch and a strong light for reading, was not so interested in a bunch of bugs, and heat, and smoke. But when I asked, "Mom, will you go over to Fuller's, and buy some graham crackers, and marshmallows, and chocolate bars? We're going to have s'mores tonight," she smiled a tremendous smile and hugged me.

They did not know, my daughters and nephew and niece, the significance of the campfire for me. But they did not have to. I knew.

None of us knew then, the many hours—some of our best—we would spend watching old logs and sappy pinecones burn down to embers whose flickering, mysterious coals we could not get enough of.

And then, as slowly as my health had left me, it now began to return. It was as if each chunk of granite I had carried to that small circle by the pond held something healing within it. Some radiating power. At least that's how it seemed to me.

At the end of the summer, we moved back home to the city for the girls' school and real life. I took up swimming. The warm water of the small therapy pool at the Y was what I preferred, but I needed the brightness of the morning light in the big one, so that's where I usually swam. Plus, I liked to be near the gals. That's what they called themselves, the members of the senior ladies aquatic aerobics class.

Most mornings when I arrived, they were already in the pool, adjusting to the water before their class began. They chatted, and waded through water up to their loose armpits, hairdos protected with baggy shower caps.

I walked slowly down the stairs into the pool and smiled as I walked past them to the lap lanes. My first lap was always cold. Made me clench. But by the third lap I was warmed. The morning light caught the bright spray of bubbles I blew into the water, expelling all that ached. It was as if I were watching illness leave my body.

I entered the pool, those mornings, as stiff as the old ladies. But I'll bet I looked young to them, and healthy, no doubt. Serious about swimming, what with my Speedo swim cap, my goggles, and all those uninterrupted laps.

But what they didn't know was that they helped me. The gals. They gave me courage. Each morning.

They called out greetings to each other, "Morning, Theresa," and "Morning, Ruthie." "Has anyone heard from Betty?" "What did the doctor say, Virginia?"

And they walked through the water lifting their arms in big circles and little circles, and laughed, and made jokes, while the young aquatic aerobics instructor played songs from *The Sound of Music* and urged them to reach higher. Higher.

Every day I swam my laps and looked up at them at each lap end. By the time I finished my routine I was loosened, warmed, and ready, like them, to begin the day.

I observed them as we all changed in the locker room. The ones who hid behind their towels, behind the curtained stalls. All that modesty seemed to make it hard to get your underpants on.

I watched others unconcerned with nudity, with their aging bodies. All those beautiful, womanly bellies. They were a parade of confidence I gleaned from.

My favorite was the oldest woman in the class who leaned on her walker, pulling her tired, purple-splotched legs toward the showers. Afterward, she wiped a towel as best she could over her back and the enormous moles I hoped someone was keeping an eye on. She had a joke or a concerned inquiry for everyone. She was joyful in a way I wanted to be. Not false. Not pretending. Just glad about life, even at her slow pace.

They were teaching me—my new swimming friends, whose names I didn't even know—a measure of gladness too.

It took a few more months before I could drive long distances again. Carry a load of wash from the basement. Go to the grocery store and buy strawberry yogurt and orange juice. Months before I came back fully to my children as their mother. But I came back.

It has been a few years now since the worst of my illness. I recovered from ten months of chronic fatigue syndrome. I have figured out ways around the fibromyalgia, one of those chronic immune illnesses the doctors tell me I will always have. Mostly these ways work.

The other night I was sitting around our campfire with my girls. Elizabeth, now taller than I, her tall mother, sat with the hood of her sweatshirt pulled tight against the mosquitoes. She was trying to get through *A Tale of Two Cities;* but Dickens was too dense for her.

She was irritated by her younger sister's attempts to play, "Praise God from Whom All Blessings Flow," on a wooden flute. She was irritated that the mosquitoes seemed only to be going for her.

I told Jennie to put away the flute, and come over and sit on my lap. As she did, I thought about how she was growing, changing, and this might be the last summer she would eagerly climb on my lap and snuggle in.

"Mommy," she said to me, a bit heavy on my lap though I was trying not to notice, "I love you so, so much."

Elizabeth rolled her eyes and pulled the cord of her sweatshirt tighter. I laughed because I know what it is like to have a younger sibling who is too adorable sometimes. She laughed too and I winked.

"And you know," Jennie said, picking up a long stick and poking around the sparking logs, "I *really* love a campfire. Aren't they just so . . . so interesting?"

I leaned back against the Adirondack chair, where three summers ago I had barely been able to lift my head. I hugged my youngest daughter and her changing body to mine and said, "A campfire, Jennie Caley, is a very good thing to love."

Elizabeth smiled and put down her book. It was getting too dark for small print words. I asked her to harmonize with me on a song and she did, as sure of the complementing notes as my mother had always been. My father would have loved it.

It was getting late. We were sleepy. I didn't want to end the night yet, but I was cold. It was still early summer in New Hampshire. Night temperatures drop quick. I rested my feet on the chunks of granite, which had collected the strong heat of our campfire. The first bat swooped down toward us, beginning the pattern the night would bring to us again.

I watched the campfire with sleepy eyes. I watched each rock that encircled it as if it were a little poem. A poem about returning to the pond and hills and trees of your childhood when you most need them. About finding what you have always found there—healing.

Each rock contained the experience. And told of it again.

# CHAPTER TWENTY-ONE

# Beyond the Altar Call

MY FAVORITE PART OF CHURCH was this: almost at the end
of the hour, after the opening hymns, after the passing of the
wooden collection plate, and after the endless sermon with its
accompanying tears—the altar call.

The preacher would invite us all to bow our heads with him
and close our eyes. He would say that he knew there were those
out there who did not have Jesus in their hearts and who
wanted to start a new life that very morning. He knew Jesus
was reaching out to us even as he spoke. The piano player
seemed to know too, and would begin the soft and loving
chords of the invitational at just the right moment each week.
We would join in and softly sing, "Just as I am, without one
plea, but that Thy blood was shed for me, and that thou bidd'st
me come to Thee, O Lamb of God, I come. I come."

What more beautiful prayer do any of us form in our hearts
than to be allowed to come into the presence of God, just as
we are? That's okay with Him. Sunday morning is slipping away

as quickly as the verses of the hymn. "And now will you please join me in singing verse three," the preacher would call, "Just as I am, though tossed about, with many a conflict, many a doubt, fightings and fears within, without, O Lamb of God, I come. I come."

I was so moved by it all—by the preacher's ability to see into our hearts, the lull of the chords, and the promise that we get to come just as we were—that I would ask Jesus into my heart every single week, just to be sure it took. When the preacher would ask for a show of hands of who had prayed the prayer with him, I would lift mine slowly and he would nod. I saw no harm in reinforcement. Nor in secretly looking around to see who else might be getting their name written in the Lamb's Book of Life at just that moment.

When we were kicked out of the church, I knew they took a part of God away from me. They took the brand-new church building my Dad had helped to build, they took the congregation singing beside me, the people who loved me, and the right to belong. But they couldn't take Jesus from my heart.

He promised He would stay with me if I only asked. And particularly since I had asked about thirty-nine times, I trusted that He had heard me.

My parents quietly helped in their own way to keep Him with us. Even though we no longer belonged to a church, my parents never stopped loving God. They sang our family's favorite hymns on every car trip we ever took, and sat with us as we said our bedtime prayers. We had a plaque hanging over our kitchen table that reminded us, "In all your ways acknowledge Him and He shall direct thy paths." It got so dusty sometimes you couldn't quite make out the words, but we never did take it down.

And when, many years later, I came to be a mother myself, I taught our girls my parents' favorite songs so that they know every verse to "I Come to the Garden" and "The King of Love My Shepherd Is," and "My Sheep Know My Voice." I give them the best of what my parents gave me.

But at times I have feared for my children's relationship with God. How could they really know Jesus if they didn't sing, "Just As I Am" at the end of the service each week? I know that our relationship with God doesn't depend on how we set up our service. And yet. There are some moments—so vulnerable and precious and important—that seem only to happen in a church that has an altar call. There's a part of me that won't quite rest unless God lets Billy Graham live long enough to do one more crusade in New England.

Maybe I need to rely more on God and less on the ways I think we get to God. To stay clear of the trap that there is only one, exact way it happens.

And so I find myself worshiping with my husband and our girls in an old, stone Episcopal church in the middle of the city, far from the plain wooden pews of The First Church of God. Far from the harmony of a gospel hymn. From the tearful plea. There is a certain stately, Episcopalian disdain for things too emotional. And perhaps, for me, this is the safer place for now.

I've been attending All Saints for seventeen years and yet it sometimes still feels new. Why do I still even go to a God church? Why don't I just go Unitarian, or skip church altogether and enjoy the leisure of the jazz brunch?

Because I need Him. It isn't just community I'm seeking. I'm seeking God. The God I was brought up on. And the more complicated God I'm coming to know. The God I belong to. No matter what anyone has ever said.

So each week, with the gentle order of the liturgy to guide me, I give it another try.

And I go to All Saints because it doesn't matter if I'm good or if I'm not good. (If you break the rules you get to try again.)

I go because at my church it is not about the individual power of some pastor or priest or prophet. It is about some words that have been around a long time. And I like words. I like stories. Especially a story that isn't always clear, that has a contradiction or two—just like me—so I love the Bible. I'm not one to toss it aside as outdated or mistranslated. I need and count on the fact that it's an ancient mixture of what is most human and most godly.

I go to church because someone will read me an old poem that's been read a lot of times before and I like old poems. And the choir will sing a psalm of the shepherd, David, who grew up to be a king, and he was good and he was not good, just like me and God still called him his friend. I like that part a lot.

And then someone reads from one of Paul's letters and I can have my usual struggle with Paul. But there is room for both Paul and me at my church.

And then the priest holds up the Bible and he doesn't look around at each one of us and smile or not smile. It isn't about whether he likes us or not. He carries the Bible slowly, slowly right out into the congregation and stands with us because, as you may remember, *the word was made flesh and dwelt among us.* And each week in that simple, slow act of the procession we are reminded again of His longing to be with us wherever we might be.

The priest chants the gospel and it doesn't matter if it's with a good voice or a bad voice. It's not a performance. It's an anonymous voice telling us again what Jesus said.

And it is this anonymity. This sameness. The ancientness of it. That's what satisfies me.

I like that no one talks to each other a lot before the service. It's not a party. People get on their knees and try to be still.

The prayers of the people we recite were written so long ago, so very long ago, that you don't get stuck with that loud lady in the back always giving her prayer needs like they are the only ones that matter. You get to silently add your own. Everybody does. I pray for my husband and our girls. My mother. My brothers. Their families. For the people of my town. And for my cousins and friends.

And there are no surprises—that's what I'm trying to say—no Bible throwing, no scary prophecies that suggest you are not quite up to ecclesiastical snuff. There are no surprises, only the quiet, precious reassurance each week: *I am with you, always. I don't change.* It amazes me every time I hear it. And it is all I need.

# CHAPTER TWENTY-TWO

# Church
# and Barns

FOR THIRTY YEARS I SEARCHED for a safe place to worship.
Now that I seem to have found it, I wonder how it is that I am
so at home in the vast stone building with its peculiar liturgy I
was not brought up to understand or to need.

But one morning, as I knelt there to pray, I understood. It
was not just a church I had entered, but also a barn. Someone
had left the high windows open and a small bird swooped
down, looping in the high air the way so many barn swallows
had in my childhood.

I saw the vaulted ceiling as hand-hewn beams arching the
barn roof. The high altar pointed east, as did our largest barn
door, and the long, wide aisle leading to it was nothing but an
immense expanse of barn floor. The side chapels were like
pens, as if each were holding a little universe of horse and goat.

I genuflected, sat down, looked around and almost laughed
out loud. The priests had taken their places in their stalls. Their

stalls—that's what they're called. I did laugh and a priest looked out dourly at me, not unlike a chewing cow.

I saw the sun coming in the windows and watched the incense rising, representing our prayers ascending to heaven. I thought of the way we used to throw down a bale of hay from the loft to the main floor and the way hay dust rose on a sunbeam.

My love for our barn and my longing for church seemed to meet for me in that moment. I felt a physical sense of home. Of the holy familiar.

And I feel it each time I leave my seat to walk up the long aisle to the altar, a walk that takes about as long as from one end of a barn to the other. I walk well-known steps to receive the earthly elements of bread and wine, which change in a way I do not need to understand, into the very presence of Christ.

I walk with others, like me and not like me, to answer another kind of altar call. The call to come. To taste and see. No one forces the gift. You answer by walking toward it. Down the long aisle, up the stairs of the chancel where the voices of young boys sing so high you will likely confuse the sound with birds at dawn or heaven itself, and then toward the altar rail crowded shoulder to shoulder with those in need of sustenance.

I bring myself and everything I have ever been to the altar.

I cup my hands and lift them silently and humbly to receive the essence. The priest places the bread tenderly, the way I might have fed our lambs. I taste the plainness of wafer and the mystery of Communion as I work my tongue and teeth around the gift, never quite comprehending; and never minding that I don't. God comes to me anyway.

And then the shared cup. The priest approaches, tilting silver toward my lips and my mouth fills with wine, and my head warms, and my throat, and I look up to regard the tangled vines of bittersweet wound at the base of each altar candle, at the open tabernacle, and the cross. I take in all of the richness of color and warm wine, of candles flickering in the mixture of the altar's shadows and morning light, of voices lifted beyond us toward Him. It is only a moment, but it is enough.

I feel my knees stiffen on the lumpy and hard mats where I kneel, receive, and ponder.

Then I must step away to let another come for that moment unlike any other. I push myself up from the rail, fold my hands together, and walk back, changed, toward the world where I live.

# Acknowledgments

Thank you, Lil Copan, my able editor and companion for every word. Lifelong gratitude to you.

Joseph Durepos, my agent: You are competent and fun— my favorite combination with work. I so much appreciate your seeing me through the process.

I am proud to have worked with Eric Major and Elizabeth Walter at Doubleday. Thank you for your insight and direction.

Kitchen Table Writers—so many of my best words I have written with you. Long may we write.

Thank you, Leanie Martin, Cindi and Bill Tolman, Reverend and Mrs. Copan, and Louis Mitchell for so many important kinds of support. Thanks as well to the members of the English Department at the University of Massachusetts, Boston, especially Martha Collins, Judith Goleman, Joyce Peseroff, Lloyd Schwartz, Louise Smith, and Taylor Stoehr.

Great admiration to Mary Oliver, whose words I read most

every day. Her poem "In Blackwater Woods" inspired the writing of my chapter "The River of Loss."

I acknowledge the storytelling ministry of Jerome Berryman and Sonja Stewart as it appears in my chapter "The Present."

Peter and Rob, Rich and Ronda, Ben and Emily—I love being family with you.

Love and gratefulness always to Laurel MacDonald Franz, Carole Fields, and Ruthanne Smith Mann, who accompany me through this life with friendship and faith.

Roy, Elizabeth, and Jennie—You brought goodness and kindness to my days of writing. I love you. The most.